Praise for *The Book of Candle Magic*

"Madame Pamita's expert knowledge and practical enthusiasm for candle magic shines brightly in this book. With wit and unique insight, she encourages all of us, novice and adept alike, to ignite our magical life."

—Chas Bogan, author of *The Secret Keys of Conjure*

"Quite possibly the most complete and straightforward book on candle magic ever written."

—Storm Faerywolf, author of *Betwixt & Between* and *Forbidden Mysteries of Faery Witchcraft*

"The clearest, most comprehensive, and thorough book I've ever encountered on candle magick. Destined to become the go-to book on candle magick ... I can't recommend this book enough."

—Jason Mankey, author of *Witch's Wheel of the Year*

"Madame Pamita is the real deal ... For the first time ever, she's put all the years of her experience and expertise into a single comprehensive and approachable guide that is sure to give all your candle spells blazing results beyond your wildest imagination."

—Mat Auryn, author of *Psychic Witch*

"Teaching with both simplicity and a depth, no easy feat, Madame Pamita illuminates the path of candle magick for the novice and seasoned practitioners alike."

—Christopher Penczak, author of The Temple of Witchcraft series

"If you have questions about candle magic, Madame Pamita has all the answers."

—Theresa Reed, author of *The Tarot Coloring Book*

"*The Book of Candle Magic* is a treasure trove of information, a comprehensive guide with something for everyone, from witchlets to seasoned practitioners."

—Pleasant Gehman, author of *Walking the Tarot Path*

"*The Book of Candle Magic* feels like I am swapping spells and trade secrets with a lifelong witch sister. This is the primer and reference book every candle witch needs to have on hand."

—Jacki Smith, author of *Coventry Magic with Candles, Oils and Herbs*

"Madame Pamita has provided a comprehensive, useful, and well thought out 'literary-buffet' of ways and means for the novice and adept candle-worker alike."

—Orion Foxwood, author of *The Candle & the Crossroads*

"Besides making the art of candle magic accessible, fun and compelling, this book also provides plenty of information for readers to deepen their own practice."

—Gabriela Herstik, author of *Bewitching the Elements*

"*The Book of Candle Magic* is more than a candle magic book; this is a resource for all magic!"

—Phoenix LeFae, author of *What is Remembered Lives*

"Madame Pamita has written a jam-packed encyclopedia of everything you need to know about candle magic… Definitely a book for anyone who wants to know how to use candles in their magical practices!"

—Najah Lightfoot, author of *Good Juju*

"Give me a magic book that assumes I know nothing. Give me a magic book that hands me the tools I need to survive. Give me the confidence to move forward with a spell when I'm a little afraid... Give me Madame Pamita, please!"

—Melissa Cynova, author of *Kitchen Table Magic*

"This book has something for everyone from the novice to the seasoned candle burner. I have been burning candles for decades and I learned a few new tricks I didn't know! Madame Pamita outdid herself. This will become a great learning tool."

—Starr Casas, author of *Old Style Conjure*

"Not since Buckland's iconic works on candle magic has any book been so poised to become the consummate reference defining this vital subject."

—Katrina Rasbold, author of *The Sacred Art of Brujeria*

"This is the grimoire you were looking for, to place on your altar and treasure all your life."

—Elhoim Leafar, author of *The Magical Art of Crafting Charm Bags*

Chris Strother

© Chris Strother

About the Author

Madame Pamita is a spell caster, candle maker, tarot reader, teacher, author, and a maker of magic, music, and mischief. She is the host of a popular YouTube channel called *Candle Magic Class* and a podcast called *Magic and the Law of Attraction*. She blogs on her own Parlour of Wonders Magic Blog as well as her Slavic magic blog, Baba Yaga's Cottage. She is the author of *Madame Pamita's Magical Tarot* (Weiser) and also makes magical beeswax candles which she sells at her online spiritual apothecary, the Parlour of Wonders. You can find her online at www .parlourofwonders.com.

THE BOOK OF

CANDLE MAGIC

MADAME PAMITA

CANDLE SPELL SECRETS
TO CHANGE YOUR LIFE

Llewellyn Publications · Woodbury, Minnesota

FIRST EDITION
Fifth Printing, 2021

Book design by Samantha Peterson
Cover design by Kevin R. Brown
Editing by Laura Kurtz
Interior art by Wen Hsu

Llewellyn Publications is a registered trademark of Llewellyn Worldwide Ltd.

Library of Congress Cataloging-in-Publication Data
Names: Madame Pamita, author.
Title: The book of candle magic : candle spell secrets to change your life
  / Madame Pamita.
Description: Woodbury, Minnesota : Llewellyn Worldwide, [2020] | Includes
  bibliographical references and index. | Summary: "A book on candle
  magic. Includes spells, dictionaries of symbols, and how-to instructions
  for making and using candles magically"-- Provided by publisher.
Identifiers: LCCN 2020032655 (print) | LCCN 2020032656 (ebook) | ISBN
  9780738764733 (paperback) | ISBN 9780738765242 (ebook)
Subjects: LCSH: Candles and lights--Miscellanea. | Magic.
Classification: LCC BF1623.C26 M33 2020 (print) | LCC BF1623.C26 (ebook)
  | DDC 133.4/3--dc23
LC record available at https://lccn.loc.gov/2020032655
LC ebook record available at https://lccn.loc.gov/2020032656

Llewellyn Publications
A Division of Llewellyn Worldwide Ltd.
2143 Wooddale Drive
Woodbury, MN 55125-2989
www.llewellyn.com

Printed in China

To Manfred
You are the light of my life

Contents

Acknowledgements

Creating a book is like getting together with a coven and casting a spell. It takes the energy of everyone to make the magic. The magic of this book wouldn't have been possible without *all* of the people who helped bring it into being.

First, I'd like to thank my Llewellyn family, especially Elysia Gallo, who always brought her positivity and happy, easy-going nature to the project. Thank you for giving me the wise guidance and gold stars all along the way that kept me going to the finish line, something I could never have done without you (and a deadline). Your saying to me, "This is good!" feels like winning the Pulitzer Prize!

Next, I'd like to thank my amazing team at the Parlour of Wonders: The central pillars, Marléne (and Cliché), Bridget, and Iris, you all held it together while I was locked away like a hermit in my room with my laptop, and to the extended team, Judy, Chelsea, and Romie, who kept the energy going with their love and support.

To my Magical Mastermind Group: Jim, Melinda, Ruth, Lacreya, and Janine. You got to hear me whine twice a month, "I can't get anything done! I'm writing a book!" You laughed with me, listened to me kvetch, and were my supportive magical siblings in this exciting journey. I can't wait to see all y'all's books!

Thank you to my mentor and inspiration, Judika Illes. Way back when, you asked me out of the blue, "Are you writing a book?" and that got the whole ball rolling. You and your legacy of amazing books on magic have been and always will be a huge inspiration to me! I wanna be you when I grow up! (I better get off my butt and write more!)

I also want to thank the amazing group of magic practitioners, and the magical-curious, that I am lucky enough to call my Spell Squad. You, and your thirst for knowing more about magic, are the *real* reason this book exists. Your questions during our online clubhouse meetings made me know that there needed to be a book out there that didn't just give recipes for spells, but explained why we choose a red candle and light it during a waxing moon to bring love into our lives. I love each and every one of you so much! I can't overstate how much I appreciate your curiosity and the brilliant questions you bring to the table every time we gather (And, if you are reading this and aren't in the Spell Squad, what are you waiting for? You can get into the club just by going to spellsquad .com).

Finally, all my extra-magical sparkly love goes to my partner, Manfred and my kids, Morgan and Miles. Thanks for letting me off the hook, giving me the space to write in every train and airport as we traveled, helping with the chores, letting me blast the cheesy sixties lounge music while I wrote, catching all those missing Oxford commas, and just being amazing humans I am so fortunate to have in my life.

And one last thank you goes out to Glinda the Good Witch Kitty, who came down in her pink bubble into my life while this book was being written. I am so lucky to have such an adorable and magical fur baby in you.

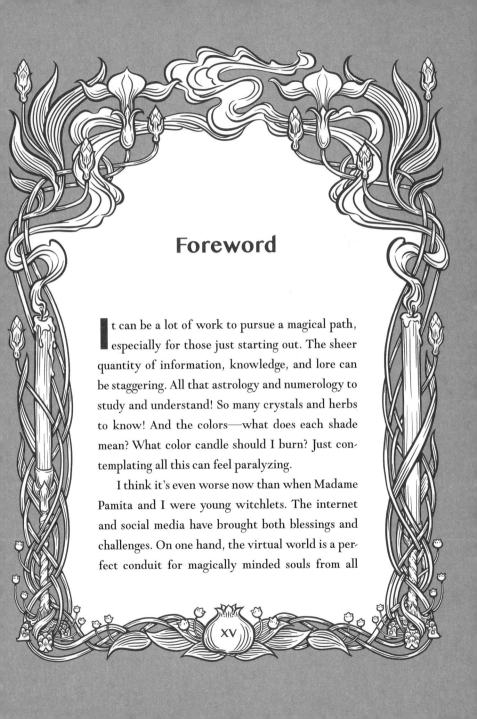

Foreword

It can be a lot of work to pursue a magical path, especially for those just starting out. The sheer quantity of information, knowledge, and lore can be staggering. All that astrology and numerology to study and understand! So many crystals and herbs to know! And the colors—what does each shade mean? What color candle should I burn? Just contemplating all this can feel paralyzing.

I think it's even worse now than when Madame Pamita and I were young witchlets. The internet and social media have brought both blessings and challenges. On one hand, the virtual world is a perfect conduit for magically minded souls from all over the world to locate kindred spirits and learn from each other. On the other hand, the sheer volume of knowledge, choices, and "experts" found on the internet can leave one feeling pressured to become an "expert" as soon as possible, too. It becomes easy to overlook an important component of what caused so many of us to be attracted to the occult in the first place: fun.

Not just for children or for when you're slacking off, fun is, in fact, a crucial part of magical practice. Read old witchcraft trial transcripts from the Burning Times. What are the alleged witches so often accused of doing? Having fun. During an era when the Church and conventional society preached asceticism and self-deprivation as the path to Heaven, witches were accused of dancing in the moonlight, feasting rather than fasting, and actually enjoying sex. Among the so-called tell-tale signs that identify one as a witch is boisterous laughter—the infamous witch's cackle. Even now, many little girls are warned against laughing loudly.

One of the secrets of the occult is the significance of fun. More than just a fleeting pleasure, it raises your magical energy and stimulates the growth of your own personal power. Yes, magic spells can potentially save you from all sorts of dire situations. They can help you achieve your dreams, ward off threats, and transform what appears to be your fate. Yes, witchcraft is serious stuff and there is genuinely so much to learn. However, fun is an intrinsic part of that learning process. How much easier to learn to distinguish one crystal from another, if you play with them, instead of just desperately trying to memorize them?

Which brings me to Madame Pamita.

Sometimes you meet someone, and you immediately like them, but sometimes you meet someone, and it's as if you *recognize* them, too. It's as if you've known each other before, although you can't recall when. That's how it was when my path first crossed Madame Pamita's.

I pride myself on having a good memory. Having been a front row witness to my father's descent into dementia, I am now extremely vigilant regarding my own mental processes. I have very distinct recollections of conversations Madame Pamita and I had very early in our friendship—she was on her way to Findhorn and I wished I was going, too—but, try as I might, I cannot recall our first encounter, other than it was on social media. This frustrated me when I first began writing the foreword to this wonderful book and so I called Madame Pamita to see whether she could jog my memory. Her recollections were as fuzzy as my own. We both agree, though, that when we "met," we were already friends.

Madame Pamita and I are bookends, born on either end of the 4th of July, united by our love of music and magic, as well as our wanderlust. Our personal friendship eventually became a professional relationship: I was blessed to edit her marvelous book, *Madame Pamita's Magical Tarot: Using the Cards to Make Your Dreams Come True* and I am so grateful, blessed, and honored to participate in this book, too.

If you have already read her work, taken her classes, or been entertained by her music, then you, too, have experienced Madame Pamita's own deep magic. For newcomers, you are in for a treat. Let me introduce you to my dear friend Madame Pamita, a true master of magic. Not just of the facts and theory, although she's definitely a master of these, too, but also of magic's inherent joy and fun. If these have been in short supply for you, let Madame Pamita rekindle your spark.

Madame Pamita is no one-trick pony. She is a well-versed adept, who is highly skilled in numerous aspects of the occult from divination to spellcasting, but especially candle magic. If you have never seen the candles that Madame Pamita designs and crafts, you owe it to yourself to take a look. (If you've never heard her sing, you owe yourself a listen, too, but that's another story for another time.) Madame Pamita is a personal repository of candle magic secrets, which she so generously shares in this book. If you are new to candle magic, this book is a great place to start—clear, lucid, and straightforward, and, yes, fun. Even if you are already a candle master, you will discover new spells and perspectives in this exceptionally complete book of candle magic.

Judika Illes, author of *Encyclopedia of 5000 Spells*
and other books devoted to the magical arts

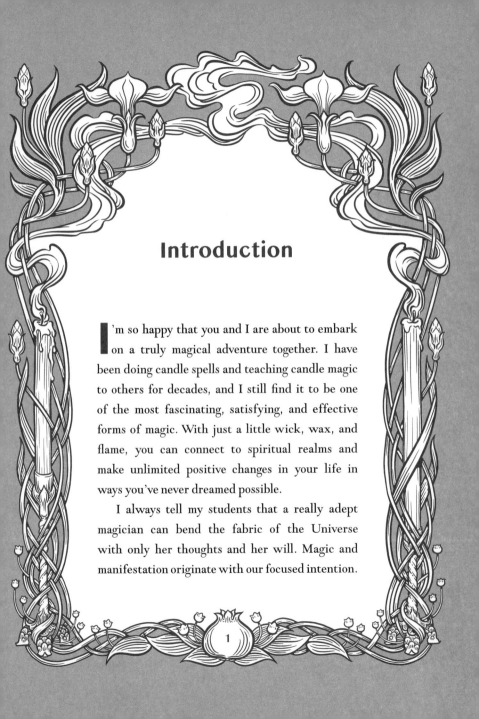

Introduction

I'm so happy that you and I are about to embark on a truly magical adventure together. I have been doing candle spells and teaching candle magic to others for decades, and I still find it to be one of the most fascinating, satisfying, and effective forms of magic. With just a little wick, wax, and flame, you can connect to spiritual realms and make unlimited positive changes in your life in ways you've never dreamed possible.

I always tell my students that a really adept magician can bend the fabric of the Universe with only her thoughts and her will. Magic and manifestation originate with our focused intention.

That pure intention *alone* can produce miraculous results. However, most of us need support in our magic to counteract the forces that work against us, namely the doubts and fears that we carry inside. That's where candle spells shine. Even if you don't have complete confidence in your intentions, your little flame will keep the positive energy moving toward your goal.

This book is a complete guide to candle magic and will not only help you understand the basic principles so that you can get started doing a spell today, but it will also help you deepen and enrich your work. Jump in and try some simple spell work, and I'm sure you'll fall in love with the magic of the flame just as I have.

You don't need to learn big, complicated spells to make magic happen. Sometimes keeping it simple and focused will lead to as good or better results than a thirteen-day moving candle spell that involves seven different candles carefully arranged in a heptagram. However, the more options you know how to use, the more customizations you can make. When you have the knowledge to bring in more elements (e.g., numbers, symbols, and colors) you have the ability to do spell work to address even the most specific details of your intention.

As easy as throwing a frozen dinner in the microwave, pretty much anyone who can strike a match can light a prepared vigil candle for a wish. However, if you take the time to plan a spell of your own design, use a figural candle, dress it with oils and herbs, choose support candles of an additional color, dress those with *different* oils, arrange them in a particular layout, and focus on your work over the course of several days, you will add *lots* of energy to your spell and probably create a more powerful and positive result. Each one of those elements adds a little push of support for your intention, and all those little boosts add up to some powerful magic.

My clients sometimes say to me, "I need your strongest spell," which is where I gently remind them that there really aren't such things as "strong" or "weak" spells, but there *is* what is best for your situation. A single candle may be all you need for a simple situation, but if you have a complicated problem that needs solving or you have a lot of specifics you'd like to add to your intention, a more complex spell working will bring you more satisfying results. In this book you will discover how to do both simple and complex work as well as how to decide what's best for your spell.

There are other reasons why you might want to do a more involved spell. Complex candle spells can be more beautiful—they can look and feel more magical, you get more involved in the spell working process, and most importantly, you learn about magic and how it works by doing more elaborate workings. Going back to our food analogy, you *could* live your whole life on microwaved dinners (I wouldn't recommend it), but learning to cook a lovingly prepared, beautifully presented meal can be really satisfying. When you can prepare that meal without following a recipe, *then* you are a chef! This book is designed to get you to "chef" level. Yes, there are a few spell recipes in here, but those are just examples, like watching a cooking show on TV. What this book is really designed to do is get you to a place where you know enough about the craft of candle magic that you can design your own spell, confidently customize each element, invent your own recipes, and see the results of that work fall beautifully into place.

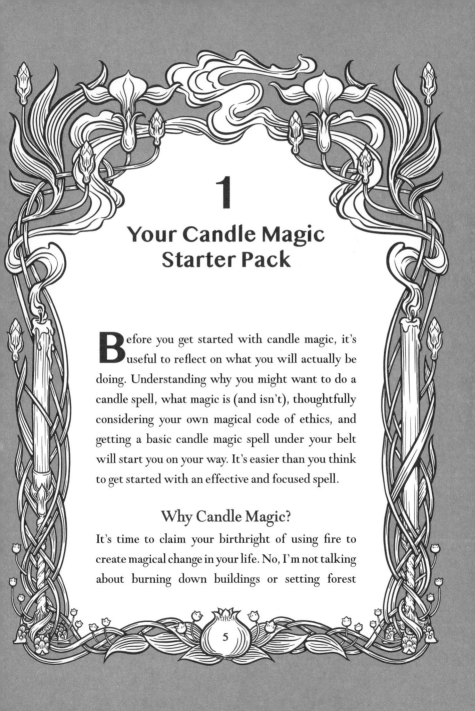

1

Your Candle Magic Starter Pack

Before you get started with candle magic, it's useful to reflect on what you will actually be doing. Understanding why you might want to do a candle spell, what magic is (and isn't), thoughtfully considering your own magical code of ethics, and getting a basic candle magic spell under your belt will start you on your way. It's easier than you think to get started with an effective and focused spell.

Why Candle Magic?

It's time to claim your birthright of using fire to create magical change in your life. No, I'm not talking about burning down buildings or setting forest fires (although, yeah, those would cause some *big* changes) . . . I'm talking about candle magic. Candle magic is the key to creating powerful rituals that rocket your intentions toward your magical goals.

Nowadays, we are able to casually turn on a gas burner or flick a lighter without a second thought, but the ancients understood the awesome power that came with having control over fire. Controlling fire transformed humans from just another species of wild animal to masters of their destiny. With control of fire came power.

Fire itself is inherently mythical and magical, and it's older than recorded history. Every time you light a candle, you connect to your oldest ancestors and their deep wisdom about fire's mystical power. Candle spells are *indeed* magical because they help us focus our wishes, commit to our spell work, and give power to our intention.

In magic, we often like to classify things as falling under one of four elements: air, fire, water, earth, and sometimes the additional fifth element of spirit. The element of fire represents action, will, and creation. Fire has the ability to rage through our lives like a devastating forest fire, or gently warm us like a campfire. Fire creates change.

It's no wonder that fire has been a part of magic for eons. Look at every early culture and civilization and you'll find fire in legends and myths. Candles are our connection through history and across cultures to the pure essence of fire's ancient force. When we make magic with candles, we connect to our deepest primal self—our magical self.

But fire isn't the only method of doing magic. Why choose candle magic over burning incense, applying oils, creating talismans, sewing poppets, making spell bottles, drawing sigils, chanting spell words, or brewing potions?

Lighting a candle for a magical purpose is like shooting off a rocket of power toward your goal. Candles have energy and force and pack it all into a limited time span. Unlike something like a charm bag that you may carry with you every day for a year or more, a candle spell packs that punch into a "right now" time frame. If there is something that you need to manifest quickly or you need some immediate change, then a candle spell will push things through with its own particular intensity.

Another special thing about candle spells is that they are infinitely adaptable: they can be used for wishes and intentions or for inviting spirits, ancestors, or deities to a ritual. You can customize them to your level of magical knowledge or for your particular life circumstances. If you are a beginner to spell work, you can do a simple yet very effective spell with a single candle. If you want to bring a lot of ritual and layers of intention to your spell, you can modify to your heart's content.

Candle spells also help us focus. After all, you can't light a candle while being distracted—burned fingers will attest to that. If you have tried to do other kinds of spells (visualizations for example) and have found that you couldn't keep your mind from wandering, candle spells will help you to focus your intention on your goal.

With candle spells, we are also given an opportunity to check in on a spell's progress. By reading how a candle burns or reading its remains, we can see if there are issues surrounding our wishes that need cleaning up or spiritual redirection.

And doing a candle spell just feels so darn magical and fun. You'll feel the power within yourself every single time you prepare your spell, speak your spell words, and light up that candle with authority.

Can I Really Do Candle Magic?

Yes, you can. You don't need to be a high priestess or priest, initiate, witch, professional spell worker, or someone who has a ton of experience in magic to do effective candle magic and get positive results. While learning under master teachers or being a serious student of a certain spiritual path will bring its own rewards, it's not required to do candle magic. Magic is true personal empowerment. Just as with art, you can go to art school and get a master's degree or be a self-taught artist—both paths lead to the creation of beautiful art.

The Seed of All Magic

If you are ready to be a serious spell caster, it's worthwhile to cultivate what I consider the seed of all magic. Everything created on this earth by humanity has started out as a thought. Mull that over for a moment. If you are sitting on a chair as you read this, that chair was designed by a person or a group of people who came up with the idea of its look and feel, the materials that would be used to make it, and its manufacture and sale that allowed you to be sitting on it right now. The chair came to be because someone had the *idea* of the chair. The same is true of *all* facets of our lives. Through the seed of thought we have the ability to create our lives as we wish them to be. You get to choose whether your thoughts are "I'll never (fill in the blank here)" or "I *will* (fill in the blank here)." You—no one else—get to decide. Whether you believe you will *never* or you believe you *will* sets the course for your life.

To take our analogy in another direction, our lives are like a horse and a wagon. We sit in the wagon and our thoughts are the horse. We can let our thought-horse run in whichever way it wants to, or we can take control of the direction of our lives through the reins of our will. If you want to take your wagon to the market, you have to direct your horse toward the market. And if you want to attain your outcome, you have to use your will to direct your thoughts.

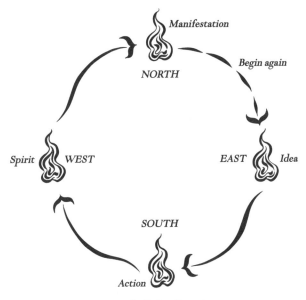

Spiral of Manifestation

Does that mean that we always have to be thinking the perfect positive thoughts at all times? Not really. It isn't that important if the horse makes a swerve to the left or the right now and then, as long as we are consistently headed toward the market. The same is true of our thoughts. If we have a moment of doubt, or a fleeting negative thought, it really doesn't affect the ultimate outcome if the majority of our thoughts are focused on the positive. Those consistent thoughts, the seed of all magic, are the beginning of manifesting all our good things and a life as we want it to be.

The process of manifestation is actually not found in any candle, herb, or talisman—the power of magic is an energy that begins within you. It starts with an idea, extends through words and actions, combines with Spirit, and becomes manifest. Once we have created the manifestation, new ideas are born; coupled with action and co-creation with the spirit world, we create even more things.

Each step is critical, and a focused and experienced spell caster can make magic without any tools aside from their mind. A magician with some spiritual awareness under her belt will focus clearly and positively on her goals, speak positive words about her intentions, take action to allow synchronicities, do magical work and trust in Spirit to align circumstances, and then wait for the culmination of those efforts. The problem is that most of us get an inner dialogue going that may sound something like this:

"I want a new love in my life . . . but everyone I meet is a player."

"I don't want to be alone . . . but I don't want to settle, either."

"I can find my true love . . . but maybe it's too late."

"I want a lover . . . but maybe I'm just meant to be single."

And around and around our minds spin like a leaf caught up in a dust devil. Where candles come in to all this is in those moments when we lose our focus or are unable to keep our mind positively on the end result without letting in feelings of doubt or disbelief. A candle spell will pick up the slack and keep the original intention going until the goal is manifested.

By itself, the candle is a neutral tool. Lighting a candle without an intention will only produce a little bit of light. The candle itself does not hold the magic. Like a blank cassette tape, you can record your intention onto a candle and it will carry that energy out into the universe.

Before you begin any spell work, first check your own thoughts and beliefs about your goals. I recommend journaling to uncover and work through any doubts. In chapter 4, you'll see how writing can help you to clear through the negative rubbish and get to the solid positive belief that will be the foundation for your amazing magical work.

Your Magical Code of Ethics

Before practicing any magic, it is essential that you contemplate your personal ethical code. As you learn about magic from various teachers and sources, you may read many different versions of ethics, many claiming that you *must* follow their code or suffer dire consequences. However, no one but *you* can decide what's right for you.

Magic isn't a religion with a set of rules and commandments. You get to decide your own rules. For that reason, I recommend reflecting on the questions below before doing any spell work. You can certainly contemplate them in meditation; however, I find it extremely effective to journal about them. Journaling helps clarify and focus thoughts and, as you grow and develop as a spell caster, you can refer back to your journal to see if you still hold the same beliefs.

- Do I belong to a religion or spiritual practice and what does my religion or practice teach about ethics?
- What does my religion or practice teach about magic or spell work, if anything?
- What are my boundaries about harm to others?
- What are my standards about controlling others?
- What are my thoughts about coercive magic (in which your wishes supersede another person's will)?
- What are my beliefs about magical responsibility?
- What is my connection to nature and the earth?

- What are my beliefs surrounding karma, "reaping what I sow," or the idea that what goes around comes around?

- What are my thoughts about doing magic on behalf of another person?

Once you have reflected on these questions, you may begin mapping out your own code of ethics. Before you begin working magically, think about what kinds of spells you are willing to do and which ones align with your code of ethics. This book is meant to be a guide on how to do magic in general, so you should be able to adapt anything found here to fit with your personal code of ethics. You might also find things in here that don't align with your code. Take what works for you and leave the rest.

A Simple Altar

Before you light your first candle for a spell, it's a good idea to determine where you are going to put it. Setting your candle in a special place adds to your magic. When we treat our candles with reverence, we are telling the Universe that what we want is important to us. An altar is one option for a space that can be set up as a focal point for prayer, meditation, or magic that we will explore more in chapter 12. For now, clear a space that will be special and safe—on a table, nightstand, or windowsill—to be your dedicated magic-making area. Make sure that the area is clear of anything that can catch fire (e.g., curtains, papers, or shelves above) and that you can keep an eye on things.

Charging a Candle

When first starting with candle magic, you may have trouble believing that what you are doing is going to have an effect on your situation. Confidence in spell work comes from experience, which is why many inexperienced people will hire experienced spell workers to cast spells for them. While no one may care more about the outcome of your spell than you do, an experienced spell caster does not have any doubts that might interfere with the outcome of the spell work done for you.

Before doing your first spell, there are some quick experiments that you can do to demonstrate that there are differences between a charged candle and an uncharged candle. When taking your first baby steps in candle magic, it's useful to be able to see these differences. Remember that the candle itself has no power—it is only a tool holding the imprint of the power put into it so that together you can manifest your intentions in the real world.

My colleague, Janine of Key & Clover, suggested the following beautifully simple experiment that can be used to note the difference in energy in a candle spell. In it, you compare the burn of a candle when it has been charged with your intention and prayer against one that has not been charged with your energy.

 Candle Charging Experiment

YOU WILL NEED

Two birthday candles

Small dish

Matches or lighter

In the following exercise, you will observe the difference between a candle you have energetically charged and one that has not been charged.

In your high school science class, you might have learned that the procedure for doing an experiment is having two components: one called the control (not modified), and one that is the variable (modified). The experiment itself is the comparison of the two. In this experiment, you are going to charge one candle and leave one candle unaffected and see the difference in how they burn. You won't be doing a spell in this experiment; instead you will simply infuse one candle with your positive energy and leave the other as is (although we *could* say that this is a spell for continued contentment).

Take two identical birthday candles from the same packet and set them on a table. Close your eyes and rub your palms together until you start to feel some warmth between them. Hold your palms a few inches apart from each other and notice the sensations you feel. Now, pick up one of the candles and hold it between your palms. Close your eyes and focus your thoughts in a positive direction. You can visualize a positive time in the past, focus in a confident way on future dreams, or just count your blessings in the present. Feel energy radiating from your hands into the candle. The important part of this experiment is to hold your intention positively, confidently, and without doubt or fear.

If you have a hard time with visualization, you can repeat affirmations that reinforce positivity, such as "I am happy" or "Everything always works out for me." You can also simply feel a sense of well-being, contentment, and peace. If your life is in a state where it's hard to feel those good feelings, then sitting down and writing a list of things that you can be grateful for in your life right now would be a great place to start.

Whatever you do, don't skimp on this part. Spend several minutes holding your candle and loading it up with positive energy. If you get distracted, put the candle back down and rub your hands together again. When you get the sense that you are complete (and you have held the candle for at least a few minutes of focused energy), the experiment can begin.

Affix both candles to a dish. If you are using beeswax candles, and the weather is warm, you can affix them by pressing them onto the dish; otherwise, slightly warm the dish or use a match to melt just a bit of the bottom of the candles and affix them to the plate.

Now, light both candles and observe how they burn. If you have made a real effort in infusing the one candle energetically, you will see a difference in how it burns. Often people report that the candle burns with a stronger flame, a flame that is more active, or that the charged candle burns faster than the control candle.

The Basics of a Candle Spell

Having seen how energy affects a spell working, it's now time to walk you through a basic candle spell so that you have a framework and can feel confident as you start on your candle magic path.

For the simplest candle spell of all, all you need is a candle, a match, and your clear intention. In fact, this was the type of candle magic I did when I was first doing spells in my childhood—setting up a candle, speaking my wish or intention out loud, and lighting my candle as I did so. If you haven't done any candle magic before, I recommend starting here.

Find a candle of any kind. For this first spell, a smaller candle such as a chime candle or a tea light is a good choice so that you can jump into doing another spell soon after, rather than waiting for this one to finish.

No matter what candle you choose, it is essential that it is a new candle, not one you have burned before, and especially not one you have burned for another spell. You don't want to confuse and dilute the energetic intention!

 Basic Candle Spell

YOU WILL NEED

Candle

Candleholder, tray, or dish

Matches or lighter

Clear intentions

1. Hold the candle in your hands for several seconds or even a minute or longer while you set your intention; imagine the outcome you want or think through the words of your wish in your head. Feel your energy radiating from your hands into the candle—this feeling charges and infuses the candle with your intentions.

2. Set the candle in its holder or on its tray.

3. Speak your wish or intention out loud as you light the candle.

4. Burn the candle while you are at home and awake. If you leave the house or go to sleep, snuff the flame out and relight it when you are able to keep an eye on it.

5. Burn the candle each day until it is completely spent.

The point of a simple spell is to focus your energy and use the ritual of lighting the candle to give some power and commitment to your inten-

tion. No muss, no fuss. You can also use this simple format when working with candles that have already been dressed with oils and herbs.

Candle spells don't have to be complicated to be effective. If you have a simple request or need to do some spell work *right now* and a candle and a match are all you have, then you can follow this basic format.

Can a Candle Spell Backfire?

It seems I get asked this question at least once a week: "What if my spell backfires?" When asked this, a lot of questions are brought to mind, namely, what does it mean for a spell to "backfire?" I get the impression from the people who ask that if a spell is done "wrong," not only will they *not* get what they were aiming for, but they'll end up in an even worse place than before they started. This is patently false. Think about it—if you were trying to make a cake and added salt instead of sugar to the recipe, you would just end up where you started before you started making the cake—with no cake. You would not end up in some negative vortex of never eating again. And the simple solution to the problem would be that you would start your recipe over again from scratch.

It's the same with spell work. If you make a huge mistake and mess up your spell, then the worst you can expect to receive is . . . nothing. No big deal! There is no karmic blowback from a spell done wrong. Like a firecracker that fizzles, it just becomes a dud. If you do a candle spell and it doesn't go well, take a deep breath, dump the spell, and start over. Light another one and let your fireworks show continue with a bang!

2
Practical (Candle) Magic

E ven though we are talking about magical, spiritual, and high level woo-woo, candle magic is about the material world too. You've got a real candle with real fire and you need to make sure you're being safe.

There are also practical parts to consider. What kinds of candles there are, other items you might want to have on hand to do a more elaborate spell, and what color candle to pick are all things you will probably wonder about once you are comfortable with the simplest spells.

Candle Spell Safety

When you are working with candles, you are working with the element of fire. As with all elemental work, if the element is not treated with reverence and respect, you may have some problems. And when it comes to fire, the consequences can be quite serious.

Here are some common-sense safety precautions that you should take whenever you are doing a candle spell.

1. Make sure you are always awake and nearby whenever a candle is burning.

2. Make sure to burn candles in an area free from things that can burn, such as furniture, bedding, carpet, books, papers, curtains, fabric, or other flammable objects.

3. Burn candles away from drafts, vents, and ceiling fans.

4. Always burn candles in a well-ventilated area.

5. Keep burning candles out of the reach of children and pets.

6. Keep your candle wick trimmed to ¼" (6 mm) as it burns.

7. Burn candles in holders designed for candle use.

8. Place holders on heat resistant surfaces.

9. Keep the wax pool free from trimmings, matches, and debris.

10. Never touch a candle while it is burning. Its container can get very hot, and hot wax could drip on you.

11. Use a snuffer to extinguish a candle; never blow it out.

12. Never extinguish a candle with water. Water can interact with wax and create a fireball, cause wax to splatter, and potentially break glass containers.

13. Snuff a candle if it smokes, flickers, or the flame becomes too high. After the candle has cooled, you can trim the wick and check for drafts.

14. Keep a fire extinguisher on hand (Class B, K, or ABC) for fires that get out of control.

Types of Candles

There are so many different candles that you can use for spell work. How do you choose? Here are most of the varieties of candles you will encounter on your candle magic journey, along with their descriptions and special features.

Taper Candles

Taper candles are long slim candles. Think of the ones that you see on a fancy dining room table. They come in many sizes from the long 12" (30 cm) ones that you see in a candelabra, called tall tapers, to shorter 5" (12 cm) ones that are used in prayer services, called thick tapers. There are slimmer, smaller ones that are sometimes called chime candles, but I like to call them slim tapers. Birthday candles also fall into the category of tapers (personally, I call them "tiny tapers.") Because they come in a variety of sizes, you can choose the ideal taper size based on how long you want the candle to burn.

Tapers can be used for spells on their own, but they can also be added as additional candles to a spell when you want to bring in some extra power. They can be used as support candles, which are extra candles placed around a main candle, sometimes called the master candle. Support candles can bring additional focus and energy by adding an additional magical color or by being dressed in different oils and herbs than

21

the master candle. Tapers are also excellent for multi-day spells, either by dividing a tall taper into sections or by burning one slim taper a day over the course of a certain number of days. A single taper can also be dressed and blessed in oils and herbs and burned individually for a quick, focused spell. The advantages to taper candles are that they are readily available, come in many colors, and are generally fragrance-free so you can add your own herbs and oils to them. Most tapers are made with paraffin, but the best-quality ones are made with beeswax.

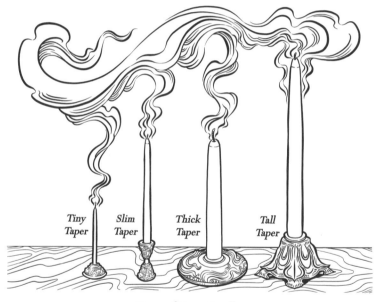

Tiny Taper   *Slim Taper*   *Thick Taper*   *Tall Taper*

Types of Taper Candles

Choose a slim taper when you want to support a bigger candle with another color or you already have a spell going and want to add an extra dose of magic. For example, if you've done a spell to get accepted to your first choice college and you're waiting to hear the results, you could light a larger candle for the college acceptance and, once that's finished burning, burn a slim taper each day to keep that energy going until you get that acceptance letter.

You can also use a slim taper or a birthday candle-sized tiny taper when you need to set off a spell immediately or almost immediately. For example, your pet just ran away and you want to send a spell immediately to enable a safe, quick return.

Pillar Candles

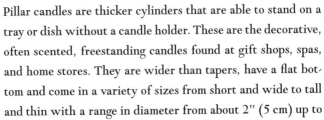

Pillar candles are thicker cylinders that are able to stand on a tray or dish without a candle holder. These are the decorative, often scented, freestanding candles found at gift shops, spas, and home stores. They are wider than tapers, have a flat bottom and come in a variety of sizes from short and wide to tall and thin with a range in diameter from about 2" (5 cm) up to 10" (25 cm) or more. Pillars come in a variety of heights too, from short and squat tea lights to tall and imposing candles that are so wide that they need multiple wicks.

Larger pillar candles are generally burned over the course of several days. The advantage to pillar candles is that they are large enough that they can be inscribed with names, wishes, or even long and detailed intentions. Many pillar candles are scented with fragrance, which can work like incense to imbue a space and be a carrier for your intentions. When looking at scented candles for magical purposes, the best ones contain some essential oils and herbs that can support and strengthen your intention. Smaller pillars and tea lights can be used like small tapers when you want to do a quick spell or burn one candle each day over the course of many days.

Vigil Candles and Jar Candles

 Vigil candles (sometimes called novena candles or sanctuary candles) are tall beeswax or paraffin pillar candles encased in a slender glass jar. These are the large candles seen in Catholic churches where parishioners can make an offering and light a candle for their prayer. At one time, they were only seen in Catholic churches but are now available in botanicas, meta-physical stores, and even in supermarkets.

Originally, they burned for nine continuous days ("novena" comes from the Latin "novem" meaning nine) but now, with manufacturers looking to cut corners, they have been made skinnier and smaller, typically lasting five to seven days if burned continuously. These candles are usually fragrance-free and can be found in many colors. When purchased at a spiritual shop, they may be purchased plain or "dressed and blessed" (sometimes referred to as a "fixed" candle), which means that the shop has added spiritual oils and/or herbs aligned with your spell work.

The glass holders of novena candles can be plain or they can be silk-screened or have paper labels with words or images on them. There are also candle refills, called pull-outs, that can be added to empty glass holders. Images and words on the glass of a vigil candle give even a novice buyer a clue as to how the candle can be used. For example, a candle with a label that says "True Love" is obviously one that can be used for love spells. As you learn about color magic later in this chapter, you will be able to identify whether you want that love candle in pink (for sweet, romantic love) or in red (for hot, passionate chemistry).

A really magical way to customize vigil candles is to start with a candle in a plain glass jar and decorate the glass yourself with paint pens, permanent markers, stickers, or a personally-designed label made with a computer printer and sticker paper.

When purchasing a vigil candle, make sure you know whether the candle is plain or dressed with herbs and oils. More experienced spell casters may want to dress a plain candle themselves, but purchasing a candle that has already been dressed and blessed by an experienced practitioner makes casting a spell as easy as speaking words of intention and lighting the candle. In the latter case, you don't have to have knowledge of what herbs or oils to add to your spell because your trusted practitioner has done it for you.

Jar candles are candles that come in a glass container of any shape or size. They can be made of beeswax, paraffin, soy, palm, or gel wax and generally come with a fragrance added. You can find this type of candle at any gift shop, spa, or home store and most are simply used to scent a space. However, there are magical varieties that incorporate herbs, essential oils, and even gemstones for magical purposes.

Votive Candles

 Votive candles are small pillar candles meant to be placed in small glass containers (traditionally red) and are essentially a smaller version of a vigil candle. Unlike vigil candles, votive candles and their glassware are often sold separately. These smaller candles were originally found in Catholic churches. A visitor to the church could make a small donation and light one instead of the larger novena candles. Votive candles usually burn in a matter of hours and are thus considered one-day spell candles; like smaller tapers and tea lights, they can be used for multi-day spells where one candle is burned per day. Many votive candles are scented, which can enhance their intent. The best candles for magical purposes, however, are loaded with essential oils and herbs to offer specific support for your spell. Plain ones can also be dressed and blessed by the spell caster. It is *not* typical to find a votive that is custom dressed and blessed on the spot like a vigil candle.

Figural Candles

 Figural or image candles are candles molded into representational shapes, such as human figures, angels, cats, pyramids, and many more symbolic styles. Figural candles are like visual talismans that add an extra degree of support to spell work. Just like a horseshoe is more than a U-shaped piece of iron, a figural candle offers a symbolic focal point and more juice to your spell through the visual image.

Figural candles are generally made with plain, unscented wax and therefore are more empowered magically when dressed with oils and herbs. They can be burned for spell work by themselves, alongside other figural candles or with taper candles used for support.

Floating Candles

 Floating candles are small figural candles shaped so that they can very prettily float in a bowl of water. Floating candles are generally made with plain wax; when used for spell work, they should be dressed with oils and herbs.

The unique feature of floating candles is that they can be floated in special waters, such as holy water, water that has been charged under a full moon, water that has been infused with herbs, or water with gemstones and talismans added to the bowl. Floating candles don't have to be floated in water, however. They can be burned on a dish or tray just like a regular figural candle.

Double-Action Candles

Double-action candles are special extra-large taper candles that have been poured or dipped so that half the candle is one color (red, green or white, for example) and the other half is black. These candles are like burning two spells in one. The black half is burned first to send any negativity back to its source and the white, red or green half is burned afterward to bring in blessings.

Triple-Action Candles

Triple-action candles are like double-action candles except that they have three colors, with the top, middle, and bottom thirds all different colors. These extra-large taper candles often start out as candles of one color and are dipped in different colors at each end to create the tricolor effect. Each color is burned for a different aspect of a single spell. They are similar to the multi-colored double-action candles in that you can incorporate more than one intention into a single candle spell. Also like double-action candles, you can use each section for a different facet of your wish. Triple-action candles can also represent any of the divine trinities, such as the Triple Goddess or the Holy Trinity and can be used as altar candles, spirit candles, or blessing candles used to invite these deities to assist in your spell work.

Reverse-Action Candles

Reverse-action candles are colored candles (usually red) coated on the outside with a layer of black wax. These candles are used to reverse negativity and send it back to where it originated. These are usually extra-large taper candles but they can sometimes be found in figural candle shapes, which can add a symbolic dimension to spell work.

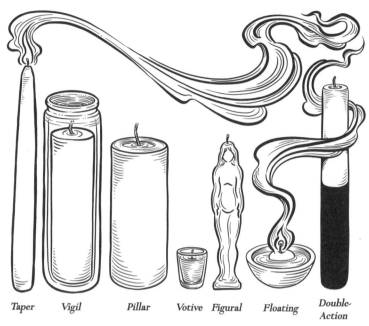

Taper   Vigil   Pillar   Votive   Figural   Floating   Double-Action

Types of Candles

Other Multi-Colored Candles

It's also possible to purchase vigil candles in multiple colors. Two, three and sometimes up to seven different colors of wax are poured layer-by-layer into a glass container. These multi-colored candles can be used to address more than one issue in a single spell. For example, you might find a Road Opener candle with layers of orange, green, and yellow wax for opportunity, prosperity, and luck respectively.

Some figural candles also come in multiple colors. These multi-colored candles can also be used for bringing different elements to one spell, e.g., a half blue and half pink skull-shaped candle (blue for reconciliation and pink for romance), or a human figure-shaped candle of red dipped in black wax for reversing.

Color Magic

Once you've determined the kind of candle that is best for your spell, you will probably start thinking about color. Color is magic! Bringing color into your spell work adds an extra dimension of support and power. When you choose a vigil candle that has a label and is already dressed with oils and herbs and blessed for a certain outcome (for example, an Abundant Prosperity candle for money or a Soul Mate candle for love), you do not necessarily have to consider the importance of the color of the candle, the candle maker has already done that work for you. But if you are choosing a plain wax candle and dressing it with oils and herbs yourself, you may want to choose a color that corresponds to your intention.

As you look at the list of colors and the corresponding areas where they are most effective, you might notice that there are a couple of issues that have more than one possible color that you can use. For example, you can do a healing spell with blue, lavender, green, or white candles. An experienced candle spell caster might notice a slightly different vibration to each color, but don't overthink things or get stuck while making a decision. Just choose the one that you feel attracted to and trust your own intuitive guidance.

Black

Banishing, transformation, uncrossing, endings, domination, protection, reversing, repulsion, freedom from evil, cursing, cloaking, sophistication, security, emotional safety, closure, breaking patterns, grief, mourning, absorbing, removing, trapping, encasing, the unconscious, mystery, shielding from the evil eye.

Blue

Reconciliation, harmony, peace, kindness, healing, ideas, intelligence, wisdom, loyalty, sleep, meditation, communication, creativity, dream work, trust, blessings, calm, forgiveness, truth, bliss, inspiration, fidelity, honesty.

Brown

Justice, balance, grounding, court cases, legal matters, being down-to-earth, practical matters, seriousness, reliability, support, stability, safety, earth, nature, animals, home, nostalgia, basic needs being met, balance.

Gray

Neutrality, neutralizing, invisibility, working in "gray areas," anonymity, hiding from others, working in-between worlds, secrets, occult and arcane wisdom, reversing, uncovering mysteries and secrets, lifting curses, undoing prior spell work.

Green

Prosperity, abundance, wealth, generosity, money luck, career, growth, fertility, gambling luck, business, a good job, harmony, balance, healing, self-love, altruism, universal love, contact with fae and nature spirits.

Lavender

Healing, calming, tranquility, spirituality, meditation, pacification, cooperation, sensitivity, compassion, empathy, selflessness.

Metallic Gold

Prosperity, fame, luxury, generosity, optimism, wisdom, enlightenment, victory, sun magic, confidence, life force, power, attraction, magnetism, vigor, charisma.

Metallic Silver

Dreams, intuition, psychic work, courtesy, honor, moon magic, rhythm, cycles, divination, illusions, glamour spells, wisdom.

Orange

New opportunities, new ventures, new beginnings, change of plans, encouragement, opening the way, removing blocks, physical comfort, warmth, security, ambition, creativity, courage, optimism.

Pink

Romantic love, friendship, soul mates, sweet feelings, emotional healing, heart connection, affection, family love, admiration, physical tranquility, nurturing, warmth, youthfulness, healing grief, compassion, forgiveness, beauty, unconditional love.

Purple

Empowerment, controlling, commanding, mastery, power, ambition, achievement, charisma, luxury, expansion, psychic ability, spirituality, authenticity, truth, transformation, insight, justice, wisdom, politics, divination, ESP, intuition, wishes, influence.

Red

Passionate love, energy, action, attraction, sexuality, magnetism, will, force, anger, fire within, courage, warmth, lust, drive, pleasure, vitality, vigor, excitement, desire.

White

Cleansing, clarity, blessing, healing, innocence, truth, connection to spirits or the spiritual world, divine connection, consecration, dream work, psychic connection, purity, rest, moon magic, angelic work, devotion, harmony, prayer, peace, purification, universal truths. White can also be used as an all-purpose color for your intention when the color you want is not available.

Yellow

Optimism, prosperity, happiness, good luck, attraction, success, confidence, visibility, fame, self-esteem, communication, concentration, focus, inspiration, intellect, logic, memory, knowledge, learning.

Candles of More Than One Color

There are also candles that are more than one color. These candles can be thought of as combining the power of two colors into one spell or as one intention (the first color burned) followed by a second intention (the second color burned).

Black and White

Reversing general negativity and bringing in blessings, invoking Mother Earth (black) and Father Sky (white), duality, yin and yang.

Black and Red

Reversing negativity surrounding relationships and bringing in love.

Black and Green

Reversing negativity surrounding money and bringing in prosperity.

Rainbow

These seven-layered candles can correspond to the chakras: red, orange, yellow, green, blue, indigo and purple or white. They can be used for chakra healing, for spells which address multiple issues or, since the rainbow is a symbol of gay pride, celebration of sexual diversity. You can

also use this rainbow candle as a seven day spell, burning one color segment each day.

Other Multi-Color Combinations

You may see a candle that has other color combinations. If you're not sure what the candle is to be used for, reverse engineer your answer. Look at the description of each color and see if they have something that connects them magically. For example, a green and yellow candle can be used for money spells—yellow for luck and green for prosperity—or it could also be used for job success. A blue and pink candle can be used for reconciliation (blue) and romance (pink). A purple and red candle can be used for power (purple) and will (red). A red, white, and blue candle can be used for vitality (red), blessing (white), and healing (blue). Keep an eye out for candles with multiple colors and think about how you can incorporate these combinations in your spell work.

What's in Your Candle Magic Toolkit?

When you are ready to do candle spell work, you will need some additional tools to prepare your candle spells. Some of these tools are a necessity and others, while optional, will add extra energy to your spells or make your candle spell casting easier and more enjoyable.

Matches, Lighters, or Eternal Flames

Believe it or not, this is a controversial topic in candle magic with pro-match and pro-lighter factions battling it out. Match lovers say that matches are more authentic, old-fashioned and ecological, while lighter fans say that the sulfur in matches will undo positive work. I have used both in my spells and haven't seen any difference in the outcome or the effectiveness of spells using one or the other, so choose whichever you feel is more magical. That being said, there are some things to think about when choosing a tool to light your candle.

Cardboard matches in a matchbook are fine if you are lighting only one or two candles, but if you are lighting more than one candle for your spell, you may want to use longer matches, such as kitchen matches, which are about 2.25" (6 cm) long, so that you don't burn your fingers. For vigil candles and candles burned in a jar, longer matches become essential to relight a candle as it burns down in the jar. Fireplace matches, which are about 11" (28 cm) long are especially useful to reach down and relight vigil candles as they near the end of their burn.

Regular cigarette lighters are not ideal for lighting candles, because you either have to turn the candle horizontal to light it or you have to turn the lighter horizontal which will cause the flame to get too close to your fingers and burn you as you hold down the spark wheel. A better option is using BBQ lighters, which are bigger cigarette lighters that have a long neck and keep the flame away from your fingers. Like fireplace matches, they are useful for reaching into tall, skinny vigil candle jars. However, the drawback to them is that most are not refillable and therefore get thrown in landfills. However, it is possible to find some refillable models; if you would like to go this route, these are preferable.

Another interesting option are USB lighters. These are reusable lighters that can be recharged through a USB plug. These lighters don't use any fuel at all; instead, they generate a small electrical spark across a gap that's just big enough to put a wick in. These also have an element of magic to them. When you zap your spell with an electrical charge, you are symbolically giving it a real dose of power. They also last for millions of zaps so, unlike disposable lighters, you won't be adding more plastic to our landfills.

Another option for lighting your spell candle is using a taper you designate as an eternal flame. While an eternal flame sounds extra special and magical, technically it just means using one candle to light another. The concept behind the eternal flame is that you don't want to use a match, which contains sulfur, or a lighter, which uses butane, to touch your spell candle. Light a taper candle with a match, lighter or with the flame of a gas stove burner and then use the taper to light your spell candle.

One last variation is good for really getting deeply into some natural magic—using a magnifying glass and the sun to start a small fire. This "sun fire" can then be used to light an eternal flame with which you can light your candle. You must have a lot of patience and a bright sunny day to do this (it's not easy), but if you want to bring the energy of the sun into your spells, it can be quite powerful and satisfying.

Glass Jars and Containers

Many candles come with a glass jar included, such as vigil candles, jar candles, and some votive candles. You might also find candles in metal cans or tins or other more heatproof containers. These containers help hold softer waxes together and let the candle wax burn completely instead of puddling and spreading out on a dish or tray. The goal with most candle spells is to burn the candle as completely as possible, so containers aid in this.

With freestanding pillar candles or extra-large tapers, I find it useful to put them in slender glass jars or larger votive holders to contain the wax and let them burn as much as possible. Burning a candle in a glass jar also allows the spell worker to do capnomancy (reading the soot or smoke on a glass candle jar) once the spell is complete.

Candleholders

A candleholder for tapers, sometimes called a taper holder, candelabra, or candlestick, can be made of any fireproof material, such as metal, ceramic or glass. A single candleholder is usually called a candleholder or candlestick, while a holder that can hold many is called a candelabra. Usually these are shaped to hold a standard taper, but slightly smaller or larger candles can be placed in them with some adjustments, either by carving the base of the candle to make it smaller or adding some soft wax candle adhesive around the base of a candle that is too small. I recommend using single candle holders when burning just one taper or in cases where you want to set tapers on an altar in a certain pattern.

There are some specialty candelabras that hold slim tapers (chime candles). Swedish brass or wooden candle holders made as Christmas decorations called angel chimes (where "chime candles" got their name) are a charming tool that could be adapted to your magic spells. These special holders feature a thin brass or wooden pinwheel that spins from the heat of the four candles below it, which also causes small chimes to ring or figures to move on a track. A menorah for Hanukkah or a kinara for Kwanzaa can also be used for spells other than honoring the seven days or eight nights of the holiday. Think about ways to use these multi-candle holders in your spell work, such as lighting more than one candle for your spell intention or lighting one candle a day over the course of several days (see chapter 8 for more information on multi-candle and multi-day spells).

Snuffers and Wick Dippers

A snuffer is a tool that "shuts off" a candle by cutting off the oxygen supply to the wick. Snuffers are often cone or bell-shaped and usually have a handle of some kind. To use a snuffer, just place the cone over the flame and hold it there for several seconds.

More than a romantic, old-fashioned way of extinguishing your candle flames, using a snuffer is also safer. Blowing a candle out with your breath always involves the risk of blowing the hot, liquid wax everywhere, creating a mess or potentially burning others. From a magical perspective, blowing out a candle shows disrespect to the spirit of fire and signals that you no longer value the objective of your spell. In many magical practices, snuffing is the acceptable way to put a spell on "pause"— blowing out a candle, by contrast, would signal the spell work is finished.

I always advise my candle magic students to snuff their candles whenever they leave the house or go to sleep. I have seen many incidents where the flames of candles have caught things on fire; if you are not there to attend to a growing flame, it can result in disaster.

Wick dippers are long metal hooks that snuff a candle by dipping the lit wick into its pool of melted wax, then gently pulling it upright so it may be lit again. While not as well-known as snuffers, they work just as well. Wick dippers are also handy for retrieving wicks that have drowned if they are caught before the wax has hardened.

Trays and Platters

If you plan on doing any complex spell work with freestanding figural, pillar, or taper candles, trays and platters are a necessity. Any tray you use for candle magic should be fireproof (e.g., no paper plates or wooden trays). You can purchase some beautiful specially-made candle trays in home decor stores or convert a baking pan, cookie sheet, heavy ceramic dish, serving plate, or platter into a candle spell platform.

Incense

While not required for doing candle magic, incense adds an extra dimension to ritual work. Our sense of smell holds our strongest memories, and I believe scent helps us focus (think of the smell of coffee or your lover's perfume or cologne). If you burn a special herbal incense that supports your magical intention in the room before you start your candle rituals, you will see a difference in the level of focus as you work.

You can also add an extra layer of magic to your spells by gently waving your candle through incense smoke before you prepare or light it. If smoke irritates your lungs, you can create a smokeless incense by putting a few drops of your favorite spiritual oil (more on that in a moment) and some spring water in a spray bottle. Shake it and spray around the room or on your candle before you begin your work.

Spiritual Oils

Spiritual oils are used to dress candles and serve a couple of purposes. First, a good-quality spiritual oil contains essential oils and herbs to support magical intentions. For example, Abundant Prosperity oil contains the essential oils and herbs (such as allspice) that are traditionally used for increasing financial abundance. In addition, oil applied to a candle creates a slightly sticky surface which helps powders, herbs, and glitter stick to the candle.

When applying oil to a candle, consider whether the spell is invoking something (bringing in) or expelling something (clearing out). If you are bringing in something, apply your oil in an upward motion from the base of the candle toward the wick. If you are clearing out something, apply your oil in a downward motion from the wick toward the base. (This topic is explored further in chapter 4.)

Spiritual Sachet Powders

Sachet powders are powders infused with essential oils and herbs to bring in a certain outcome. Think of them as spiritual oils in powder form. Sachet powders can be sprinkled around the base of a candle or applied to candles directly (if applied, they stick better if the candle has been dressed in an oil first). You can use the same oil and sachet powder on a candle (e.g., Powerful Protection oil and sachet), or customize your spell intention by mixing and matching (e.g., Magnetic Attraction oil with True Love sachet).

Sachet powders can also be sprinkled on candle trays or altars to draw magical shapes around your candle which can empower your spells. (Check out chapter 9 for more information about the magic of shapes.)

Herbs, Roots, Flowers, and Resins

Use fresh or dried plant material in your spells to add extra power and support. Herbs, roots, and flowers are the icing on your candle spell cake. You can sprinkle dried herbs on top of vigil or pillar candles; soften the wax of a pillar or taper candle and roll it in herbs; dress a figural candle in oil and sprinkle herbs on it; and/or place fresh or dried flowers, roots, or herbs on the tray around your candle spell. Refer to appendix I for a list of herbs and their magical uses.

No matter how you use herbs, be sparing with your use. More herbs do not mean a more powerful spell. Dried plant material is flammable, so don't overload your candle with herbal matter or you will end up with a fiery mess. If in doubt, use less and sprinkle your herbs around the candle, rather than on top of it. Herbs sprinkled around a candle can still catch fire but are less likely to ignite than the herbs sprinkled directly on top of your candle.

Petition Papers

Petition papers are slips of paper on which you write your wishes, spell words, or intentions. A basic petition paper is a piece of paper that is large enough for you to write out intentions but small enough to be folded and placed under your candle spell tray, candle holder, or vigil candle. Usually, a petition paper is about 2" (5 cm) square, though you can certainly experiment with larger or smaller paper or a shape other than a square.

Petition papers can be written on any kind of paper, though some people like to incorporate extra magic in their spell by using a special paper such as parchment or a colored paper that corresponds to their intention (see the Candle Color section in this chapter for guidelines on color magic). Your petition can be typed or printed on the computer, but I prefer writing my petition paper out by hand. You can use either a pen or pencil and can incorporate color magic by using a colored ink or pencil that supports your magical intention.

There are many styles of petition papers ranging from basic to quite elaborate, and we explore them in chapter 3, on writing magic words.

Gemstones, Shells, and Talismans

Crystals, shells, and good luck charms add extra magical support and beauty to a candle spell. You can add rough crystal points or tumbled gemstones around your candle to charge your spell with the energy of that gem. You can choose the gems intuitively or use appendix II to find the right gem for your spell work. There are many easy-to-find and reasonably priced gems that can support your work in powerful ways.

Shells can also be used magically to enhance your candle spell. Shells carry the energy of their home, the sea, and bring all the emotional power of the ocean to your intention. You can choose shells you simply find attractive or select ones based on your magical goals. You can also repurpose shells from a meal and use them in your candle spell work. (I love the idea of saving a magical item from ending up in a landfill.) Take a look at appendix III at the back of the book for a list of shells and their magical uses.

Talismans and amulets are natural or crafted curios that we would generally call "good luck charms." Coins, charms, and jewelry can be added to your spell to support its positive outcome. Using items that have personal significance to you, e.g., a lucky coin or a ring given to you by a lover, can add a personal connection to your spell. Commercially-made charms in symbolic shapes such as a heart or a four-leaf clover can also be added to any spell—simply place them around the candle. A list of magical talismans can be found in appendix IV.

Whatever you use, place your gemstones, shells, or talismans around the candle before burning it. After your candle spell is complete, you may carry the charms with you, wear them, or place them on your altar to keep the power of your spell going.

Glitter and Confetti

Glitter and confetti can bring color magic to your spell work (see the Color Magic section earlier in this chapter) as well as reflective energy for radiating your intention out into the world. You can use glitter of the same color as your candle to give extra support or use glitter of another color if you want to add another layer of intention to your spell. Glitter and confetti can even add another element that you can "read" once the spell is complete (See chapter 11 for more information on reading candle wax).

Keep in mind that while glitter can be a lovely addition to candle spells, most glitter and confetti is made from micro-plastics. These are somewhat problematic as they add to the pollution problem and can end up in the oceans and land where they can be swallowed by animals or take millennia to decompose. And while paper confetti might seem like a good alternative to plastic, I tend to shy away from using paper confetti in candle spells because paper can catch fire and create smoke and fire hazards.

There is some good news, though. If you are willing to look for them, there are a lot of alternatives that will let you get shiny with your spell and still remain eco-conscious. You can use biodegradable glitter (sometimes called eco-glitter) made from cellulose (a plant product), powdered mica or mica flakes (a natural mineral), glass glitter, glass beads, flat-back glass rhinestones (all made from glass), crushed gemstones, edible glitter or confetti (which is made from sugar and can be great in sweet love spells), real gold or silver leaf, or imitation gold or silver leaf (made from copper and aluminum). All of these are less harmful on the environment and can still bring amazing sparkle to your magic.

To use these in your spell work, apply oil to your candle and then sprinkle it with glitter to make it shine. You could also add a small pinch of glitter to the top of a vigil candle to bring some extra color magic.

Scissors, Wick Trimmers, and Tweezers

When burning a candle, the ideal wick length should be between ¼" (6 mm) to ½" (12 mm). When a wick is too long, it produces soot and smoke, burns too hot and quickly, and its burnt pieces accumulate in the pool of wax and can catch fire.

It's possible to trim the wick of a new candle to an acceptable length with scissors before burning, but they are a bit tricky to use while the candle is burning (especially if you are working with a jar or vigil candle). Instead, use a wick trimmer, a special pair of scissors that allows a wick to be trimmed to the ideal length, even if it's at the bottom of a vigil candle glass. The way wick trimmers are shaped also catches the trimmed pieces so they won't fall into the wax and create a fire hazard.

Here's a handy witch tip: If you trim a new candle, save those little extra bits of unused wick so that you can use them as helper wicks for a candle that has a wick that gets lost or is too short (see the section on what it means if your wick disappears in chapter 11 for information on how to make a helper wick).

It's also a good idea to have a long pair of tweezers (sometimes called "aquarium tweezers") on hand to pull out fallen wick pieces or any extra material that may land in the candle. Tweezers also come in handy to pull out wicks that have drowned in excess wax and to pinch out candle flames instead of snuffing them. They can also be used for lighting incense charcoals without burning your fingers. Find them at aquarium supply stores or online.

Nails, Pins, Wax Inscribers, and Carving Tools

Spell work requires that you sometimes play with something sharp. In the case of candles, nails and pins will come in very handy. Large nails are useful for inscribing words and names on candles. You can make these tools extra special for your spell work. For example, you can use large "golden" brass nails, copper nails, and hammered iron "coffin nails" for inscribing on your candles and bringing in all the magical power of these metals.

Some people use pins for inscribing on candles, but they are really too fine, difficult to control, and flimsy to scratch into hard wax without bending. However, pins are the perfect tool for marking off sections of candles for multi-day spells. You can use colorful glass head straight pins for marking off candle segments, but plain straight pins will work just as well.

Pins also focus power. Think of a pin marking a spot on a map. Use a pin like a mini magic wand to point at an area on a figural candle where you would like to make some change or send some concentrated energy. Many people think that using pins in this way is like using pins on a voodoo doll to cause someone harm; while you could certainly use these focal points in that way, you can also use them for good. It all depends on your intent. For example, use a pin with a pink head stuck in the heart to cause someone to feel more loving feelings.

Wax inscribers are special dedicated tools used only for carving into wax. They look similar to metal pencils and have sharp points on one or both ends. The advantage to the inscriber is that they are easy to hold and write with. You can find ones made intentionally as magical tools which can then add some extra energy to a spell.

If you like to carve symbols and sigils into the side of your pillar candle or pull-out candle, art supply stores sell many tools that can be used for carving and inscribing. Try working with linoleum cutting knives, etching needles, or a stylus for a variety of line thicknesses and detail.

Knives and Candle Tools

Knives are useful for carving candles. You may want to carve off the excess wax on a wide pillar candle if the wick burns down the center or cut channels in the sides if the wax pools in the center. You can also use knives to cut the top off a reversing candle and carve a new top out of the bottom, so you can turn the candle upside down as described in the section on double-action candles in chapter 10.

A candle tool is a long, pencil-sized metal instrument with one end featuring a pointed gouge and the other end a small scoop, almost like a doll-sized ice cream scoop. Candle tools are used to carve off excess wax or cut channels on pillar candles like a knife, but their brilliance is in the scoop end, which allows you to carve the wax around a drowned wick without cutting through the wick, so that you can revive candles that have gone out too soon.

Screwdrivers, Awls, Icepicks, Metal Chopsticks, and Metal Knitting Needles

A sharp tool such as a screwdriver, awl, icepick, metal chopstick, or metal knitting needle will be useful in dressing and blessing vigil candles. With these long, pointed objects, you can poke holes into the top of a vigil candle to dress the candle with oil by placing a drop of oil in each hole. In the case of chopsticks or knitting needles, metal ones are necessary because most wooden and plastic ones break from the force of poking the holes.

These long sharp objects also come in handy if you have to poke a hole to add a new wick to a candle in which the wick has disappeared. In a pinch, they can also be used as inscribers.

Soft Wax Candle Adhesive, Candle Snuggers, Candle Grippers, and Candle Sharpeners

If you've worked with taper candles, you start to realize that there is no standardized size for candles and candle holders. Candles can be too big or too skinny for a candle holder, or holders can be too tight or too loose. The result is a taper candle that tips over. What's a witch to do? There are many tools and materials that help fit taper candles in candle holders.

Candle adhesive is soft, sticky wax that keeps a candle firmly in the holder or fills in gaps when the candle is too skinny for its holder. Candle adhesive comes in rolls, tins, or in wax dots on a card.

Candle grips or snuggers are foam circles that can be placed on the base of a taper to fill in the gap when the fit is loose. Candle grippers are ridged rubber bands that go around the base of a candle to make a snug fit in a candle holder.

Candle sharpeners, which are like large crayon sharpeners, can be used to make the base of a candle smaller so that it can fit in a candle holder that is too tight.

Fire Extinguishers, Baking Soda, Sand, and Pan Lids

If you're burning candles at home, it's always a good idea to have a fire extinguisher, baking soda, or a bucket of sand available if a flame gets out of hand. While your instinct might be to use water to extinguish a candle gone haywire, it can actually make the fire worse—when melted wax is doused in water, it can create a dangerous fireball known as a wax fire. The best option is to use a fire extinguisher classed for grease fires (Class B, K, or ABC) or a large box of baking soda or bucket of sand to put out a fire. You can also snuff out a smaller fire with a frying pan lid.

3

Magic Words

Words are an important part of any spell. They are the element of communication and help us to clarify ideas and share them with others, whether spoken out loud or written down. In spell work, "others" can be people we are doing our spell work with, or deities, Spirit, the Universe, spirit guides, or even our higher selves.

One of the most powerful parts of a candle spell is the words you use. When you write out your intentions on your petition paper and speak those spell words out loud, you are setting the direction of your spell.

Pre-Writing the Perfect Spell Words

Have you ever had the experience of speaking before you've completely clarified your thoughts? We stumble with the words, and maybe (hopefully) get to a place where we communicate what we mean. But if we take the time to plan out our words ahead of time, we are more likely to get to the point without unnecessary confusion.

Planning out words is also great for spells. We don't want to be stumbling around for the right words when we could be committing those words to paper or speaking them aloud with authority.

Before getting started with your petition paper or your spoken spell, it's helpful to first write down your intention to gain clarity. Grab a piece of scratch paper and simply write your wishes or intentions stream-of-consciousness style for the spell. When writing, make sure you amp up your intention to its highest level. So if you are writing a wish, make it a big wish, not a mediocre one.

Write down what you hope to achieve with your spell and dig a little deeper. Do you have fears about your magic? Do you worry that your spell won't manifest or that you'll do something wrong? Do you feel as though you lack the belief that your spell can ever come true? What are the underlying feelings that you think getting your wish will resolve? These are the things that you want to explore in your pre-writing. Write it all out and get your thoughts, beliefs and feelings out there so that you can confront them and transform them. Give yourself plenty of time to focus on your feelings and allow everything you're thinking about the topic to come to the surface. If your writing meanders into other areas, that's okay. This is the freeform pre-writing stage, so whatever comes out is fine because it will be edited later.

First, start out by writing about the problem you are trying to solve in its entirety. Just write out all your thoughts, feeling and ideas as if you were unloading your problem to a close friend. An example of this freeform writing might look something like this:

I wish I could get another job. My work is really stressful. I hate my job and wish I could just quit and find something else. I feel overwhelmed by the tasks they give me and I keep making mistakes. Maybe I could start my own business on the side and just never have to go in to work again. That would be amazing. I hate going in to work. It's not that I hate the work, I like doing the tasks but my boss is making me feel like I don't know what I'm doing. He doesn't give enough time to finish the projects and he definitely has to have it his way and won't let me figure out a system that works for me. He is really nice to some of the employees and really critical of me and a couple of the others. It feels like he is really playing favorites and letting the ones that he is friendly with get away with murder, while with me he is picky about every little detail. I wish I could work somewhere else, but there are so many things about this job that I like. I have a lot of good friends here, they are really flexible with my hours and it's so close to home. The pay is really good and it would also look really good to have this position on my resume for a few years, so I don't want to have to quit and take another job right now just because of him, but he's making my work life unbearable. I just wish I had a different boss, but he's been in this position for years and isn't going anywhere. He's not a total jerk. When I see him being friendly with the others, he seems pretty nice and my coworkers seem to like him just fine. It's just not fair. Maybe if he were just nicer to me or had a better opinion of me, things would be better. If he were as nice to me as he is to the others, I feel like everything else would fall into place. I could finally like my work.

In the example, the person started out with the idea that they wanted to get another job, but by the end, they realized that the problem was not the job itself but the boss. If the boss would just stop being so hard on them, the job would be pretty good. Had the person not taken time to write things out, they might have done a spell for a new job, but free writing helped them realize that the job wasn't the problem. The spell work should focus on the boss having a better attitude toward the person.

After you have written for several minutes or a page or two of your thoughts, you're ready to go back and find the precise words that will eventually become your petition paper.

Writing Your Petition Paper

Taking the words from your pre-writing, you can now refine them and mold them into your petition. A petition paper is a written wish or intention that says what your spell is about. It can be used as a simple spell by itself or added to other magical items to give your magic a direction. Petition papers clarify the focus of the spell and empower your intention. A basic petition paper is simply the concise wording of what you want your spell to do.

When you are making a formal agreement with another person, often you will write out a contract to make sure that everyone is on the same page and that there are no misunderstandings. Written contracts also define the agreement as a serious one. I like to think of a petition paper as a contract with the Universe. You are clarifying your intention to yourself and the Universe, and you are also committing to it and saying that you are serious about wanting your wishes to come true. A contract isn't for wafflers or people who are on the fence. When you write a petition paper, you are showing the Universe that you have a serious and focused intention.

Like a good contract, a petition paper should be focused and precise. Because you are working on a manifestation, you should keep your petition paper positive—that is, write out what you *do* want instead of what you *don't* want. There are a couple of reasons: If you say what you don't want, that leaves a whole lot of options for what can come through. If you write, "I don't want an old truck" what does it mean? Does it mean you want a new truck? A car? No vehicle at all? There's a lot of room for interpretation. Likewise, when you say what you don't want, you are actually putting your focus on it. For a fleeting thought it's not a problem, but if you're intensely focused on that old truck that you don't want, you're putting your attention in the wrong place.

To make a really solid petition paper, a great place to start is to go back to the pre-writing you did and begin to edit. First, start crossing out any words or phrases that aren't focused on the ultimate goal. If you've gone off on tangents or into other areas that don't have anything to do with your goal, cross those out right away.

Next, look at the negative words that express your fears or what you don't want, cross them out and rewrite them as positives. If you wrote, "I don't want a job that pays minimum wage," write what you *do* want: "I have a job that pays me $150,000 a year." Crossing out the words and rewriting them at this stage is a powerful part of your spell. You are rewiring your brain to transform the negative focus into a positive one. The act of crossing out negates the negative and rewriting creates a new positive pathway for your intention to flow.

Now it's time to get to the point: take the essential words of your spell and combine them into succinct smaller sentences. Long phrases like, "When I get down to it, what I really want is to feel better, have more energy, be able to walk upstairs without losing my breath, feel good, look good, and be really healthy," can be transformed into the much more concise "I feel healthy." Sometimes students say to me, "But writing out just one sentence doesn't convey all the other things I want—the increased energy, the feeling better, the not losing my breath," but it *does* convey all of that. You wrote it out in your rough draft, so you know that the phrase "I feel healthy" conveys and includes all the details of what you believe your perfect health will look like.

Next, take out what I call the "wimpy words" that make your spell wishy-washy or your desire something that is coming in "the future," whenever that is! Instead of writing, "I will attract the perfect lover," make it a more forceful, "I attract the perfect lover." Instead of "I want a new car," say, "I have a new car," "I am the proud owner of a brand new Mercedes," or "The perfect car is mine."

Once you've determined your petition words, it's time to do the final draft. Choose a paper that feels good to you. Some write their petitions on brown paper, others on parchment, and still others on special fancy colored papers. There is no one paper that is more magical or powerful than any other; it's a matter of personal preference.

If you're just starting out doing petition papers, try using a variety of different types of paper to see if you like working with one more than the others. Here are some ideas to get you started:

- Parchment
- Brown kraft paper (or repurposed paper bags)
- Stationery
- Colored construction paper
- Origami paper
- Postcards
- Greeting cards
- Cardstock
- Index cards
- Decorative papers
- Photographs
- Paper money (real or play)
- Wrapping paper
- Copier paper
- Handmade papers
- Newsprint (with no printing on it)
- Wallpaper

If you can choose papers that also support your spell, all the better. Green or gold colored papers, for example, could be used for a prosperity spell. Handmade paper made with embedded sunflower petals could be used for a fame and recognition spell. A paper that was touched by a person whom you want to attract is great for a love spell.

You may also want to choose a colored ink that supports your intention or, if you want to get very fancy, ink that has been infused with herbs or resins that support your intention. An example of this is Dragon's

Blood ink, which is made with resin of the dragon tree and carries with it the magic of protection, love, and prosperity.

Types of Petition Papers

There are plenty of styles of petition papers from simple to quite elaborate. Complex doesn't always mean better, though. Try several of them out and see which ones are most inspiring to you.

Petition Paper #1

The easiest petition paper is to simply write your words of power as if you were writing a note. This is my favorite form of petition for its straightforward no-fuss, no-muss energy. In cursive or printed letters, write out your short statement in a powerful positive sentence or two. That's it!

Petition Paper #2

Write out your power sentence and add symbols that support the intention. For example, you could draw hearts on the four corners of a love spell petition paper or dollar signs all around a prosperity petition. Check out the section on symbols in this chapter or appendix V for inspiration.

Petition Paper #3

Write your power words out a certain number of times. Chapter 8 will help in selecting magical numbers that support your intention, or you can go a more traditional route and choose three, seven, nine, eleven, or thirteen times. Write your phrase over and over again, each phrase stacked on top of the other. For example, you could write "I am hired for the perfect job" four times, one stacked on the other, as the number four emphasizes your career's long-lasting stability.

Petition Paper #4

Another method of writing a petition paper is to write your power statement and then turn the paper 90 degrees to the right. With your original
statement now vertical, write your name over it horizontally, so it looks
like a cross. This kind of working is perfect for when personal power is
related to the issue at hand. For example, in certain situations, people
write the name of their target and then rotate the paper until that name
is vertical and then write their own name over the name of the other
person to have control over that person.

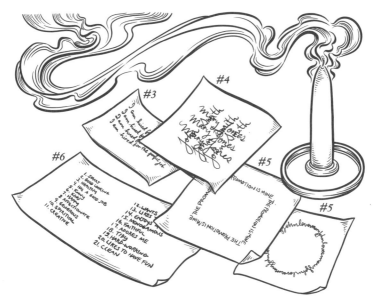

Examples of Petition Papers

A variation on this is to write your issue or the target's name a certain
number of times (as described in example 3), turn the paper so those names
are vertical and then write your name the same number of times over the

other person's name so that it looks like a grid. This is perfect for spells where you want to have some extra control over a person or situation.

Petition Paper #5

Write your words in a shape that supports the intention. Refer to chapter 9's section on shapes for ideas. If you wanted to ensure a lifelong commitment, for example, you could write words such as, "John loves Mary" over and over in the form of a circle. Or if you wanted to build a strong career, you could write "The promotion is mine" four times as four sides of a square.

One old-time method of writing petition paper words in a shape is to write in cursive, not lifting your pen from the paper and linking the end of the last letter and the beginning of the first so that the words make a never-ending loop. While a circle is traditional, this linked writing could be done in any shape. The most important key to this type of writing is that you don't dot the i's or cross the t's until after you've linked the main letters together.

Petition Paper #6

One of my favorite petition papers is what I call the Magic 21. This petition is simply a list of the twenty-one qualities of the perfect job/partner/relationship/house/whatever. Writing a list of twenty-one incorporates complex numerology that creates powerful manifestations and the fulfillment of your biggest dreams and desires. List your top 21 qualities of the thing that you want without specifically calling out a particular person, job title, workplace, address, etc.

Placing Your Petition Paper

Once you've written your petition paper, you may need to fold it to make it the right size to place beneath your candle holder or tray. If your spell's objective is to bring something to you, fold the paper toward you. If you need to fold it a second time, turn the paper clockwise and fold it toward yourself again. If your work is to banish, eliminate, or reduce something, fold the paper away from you and turn counterclockwise to fold again.

Once the petition paper is folded, place it beneath your candle dish, tray, or holder. Some people also like to place the petition papers between the candle and the holder or tray. This doesn't actually add any benefit and is not the safest method because the paper can catch fire. Placing the paper away from the flame is safer and confers the same power as placing it touching the candle.

Spoken Spells

Writing down your spell words as a petition paper is the perfect place to focus your spell and intention, but speaking those words out loud adds commitment to your outcome. When you're doing a candle spell, it's natural to want to say something as you light your candle, reaffirming the intention of your spell at the moment you set it off.

Simple Spell Words

There are a few different ways that you can speak your spell words. The easiest is simply to repeat the words on your petition paper. If you have written, "I have a beautiful new car," you can speak those same words as you light the candle. The key is to say them with power. Don't say "I have a new car?" with your voice tentatively going up with an unsure, wobbly quaver. Say "I HAVE a new car!" with power and force. You don't have to necessarily shout it; even a whisper can be powerful if there is conviction behind it. Just say it like you mean it. Act as if the car is already here and you are excitedly telling someone about it.

Improvised Spell Words

The second is to extemporaneously speak your intention with the words that just flow out of you naturally. For example, you could say something like, "The gates of the Universe open to me and the perfect new car comes to me effortlessly. I have a new car that I enjoy driving and that keeps me safe. I am able to pay for this car easily." Any positive feelings you have about this car and the process of it coming to you can be included in these stream-of-consciousness-style spell words.

Rhyming Spell Words

The third way to create spoken spell words is to craft rhyming couplets. For this method, you will need a couple of pieces of paper, one for scratch and one for your final draft.

On your scratch paper, write out several key words related to your spell. If you are looking for key words, you can refer to your original free writing or your petition, or you can come up with a whole new set of key words related to your spell. For example, you might write down the words: car, new, wheels, road, travel, safe, comfortable, fast, luxurious, and so on.

The next step is to take a few of these words and find rhymes for them (if you get stuck, you can always refer to a rhyming dictionary online). So, for "car" rhyming words we could use are bar, char, far, jar, mar, par, star, and tar. For "road" we might use the words bode, code, goad, load, node, toad. For "fast," we find cast, last, mast, past, vast.

Once you have these rhymes for your key words, choose the ones that make the most sense and seem to flow with the vibe of your spell and create a couplet that has a nice rhythm.

I know the spell, I know the code
To take me to the open road
My old car's days are finally past
My new car moves me safe and fast
The goddess gives me a new car
That's going to take me very far

The spell words don't have to be Shakespeare-level poetry; after all, no one is going to hear them but you. However, for a fun and witchy-sounding way to express those key words in your spoken spell, speaking in rhyming couplets works well.

Three Spell Word Power Boosters

Once you have your perfectly phrased words with all their power, I recommend adding the secret sauce to your spell—three phrases you can tack on to your spell words to really open up their power.

The first is to tag on "...or something even better" to your intention. For example, "I make a record that goes platinum or something even better." This phrase is perfect in the spell casting process because it allows wiggle room for there being an even better outcome than the one you are envisioning, like your record going triple platinum!

The second is to include the phrase "the perfect outcome in perfect timing." By including this in your spell words, you are opening your spell so that things come to you at just the right time—neither too soon, nor too late. I also find that repeating this phrase even after your spell has finished can calm you when you are feeling impatient or worried that things aren't moving.

The third phrase is a little more complex but will allow you to really get into your flow toward your best outcome: "a closed door is as good as an open door." What it means is that if you are trying for some particular outcome and it doesn't appear, there *are* other options. You will be able to find peace knowing that option one (the one that didn't happen) is not as good as option two, three, four, or five.

When you think of your outcome, imagine it being like the Universe is throwing you an amazing party. All your favorite people are going to be there with amazing music, delicious food and drink, and it's going to be held in a penthouse suite at a fancy hotel (so you don't have to clean up afterward!). The hitch is that you've been given the key but don't know what room it's going to be in. Your job is to try each door on that penthouse floor until one opens. The closed doors are not keeping you from your party; in fact, quite the opposite: those closed doors are just telling you "your party isn't in this room." It's nothing personal, and it's not like you are missing out on anything behind those other doors.

The place where this kind of consciousness comes in handy is when you are trying for something that has many possible options, which, truth be told, is pretty much everything in life. If you're looking for the perfect lover, the ideal job, a new apartment, and so on, you're probably going to encounter some closed doors along the way. The phrase "a closed door is as good as an open door" helps you to not get stuck at those closed doors. In the case of our party analogy, if you tried your key and the door didn't open, you would just move on—you wouldn't take a battering ram to the door or collapse in a heap and sob your eyes out at the threshold.

You may feel momentarily bad that the "perfect" job didn't open up for you or the hot guy wasn't interested in you, but the point is to shake it off, know that there is something even better for you out there, and not to take the locked door personally.

These three add-on phrases will keep you in your highest vibe magic. They will open you up to better options, help you trust the timing, and remind you that there are always other possible outcomes (and maybe even better ones).

Symbols, Seals, and Sigils

Ideas don't have to be expressed using words, necessarily. Symbols, seals, and sigils are beautiful, personal, and sometimes secretive ways to set your spell's focus to convey magical intention without words. While slightly different from one another, what they all have in common is that images, rather than words, represent the spell's intention.

Symbols, seals, or sigils can be drawn on a petition paper, inscribed in the candle wax, or drawn onto the side of a glass candle holder with a paint pen or permanent marker.

Symbols

Symbols are images that represent a concept. Symbols can be written on petition papers or petition papers can be cut out in the shape of a symbol. They can be carved onto the surface of a candle, stamped into sealing wax to make a talisman and laid next to your candle spell, or incorporated into the candle layout (see chapter 9 for more information about layouts). They can also be drawn onto a glass candle holder with a paint pen or permanent marker (paint pens are permanent and permanent markers can actually be wiped away ... go figure!).

Examples of Symbols
- Secular symbols (for example: hearts, stars, dollar signs, etc.)
- Religious symbols (for example: Pagan triple moon, Vodun veve, Christian cross, Jewish Star of David, etc.)
- Runes and bind runes
- Egyptian hieroglyphics

Seals

Sigils

Symbols

Sigils

Examples of Symbols, Seals & Sigils

- Alchemical symbols
- Planetary symbols
- Zodiac symbols

Seals

Seals are formal magical designs that have been used for centuries to invoke spirits or ensure certain outcomes. Incorporate seals into your work by purchasing seals individually printed on parchment paper, copying them from a book, or printing them out from the internet. That said, the most powerful method of working with these magical talismans is by copying them by hand.

In recent years, seals have been printed on parchment paper (a semi-translucent paper that looks like real parchment or vellum made from sheepskin), so if you are printing or making your own, you can follow this tradition or work in the way recommended by the reference you are using.

Examples of Seals
- Seals of Solomon
- Seals of Moses
- Magic Squares of Abramelin
- Planetary Seals
- Angelic Seals
- Sigillum Dei Aemeth of John Dee

Sigils

Sigils are a personal magical and symbolic representation of a desired outcome for a spell. They are usually created by the magical practitioner through merging letters (or sometimes images) into a unique personal design, although it is possible to use sigils that others have created for generic purposes.

To make a sigil, write out your intention in a phrase. Cross out all of the vowels, then cross out any duplicate consonants so there is just one of each consonant. With these remaining letters, combine them in a stylistic way to make a symbol.

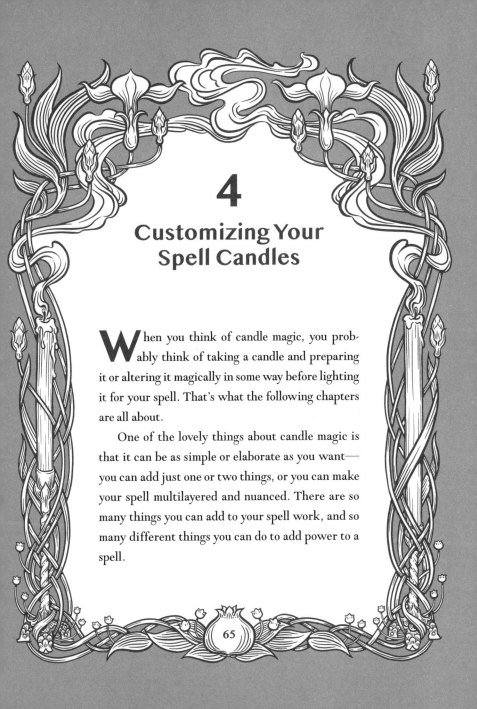

4

Customizing Your Spell Candles

When you think of candle magic, you probably think of taking a candle and preparing it or altering it magically in some way before lighting it for your spell. That's what the following chapters are all about.

One of the lovely things about candle magic is that it can be as simple or elaborate as you want—you can add just one or two things, or you can make your spell multilayered and nuanced. There are so many things you can add to your spell work, and so many different things you can do to add power to a spell.

If you're just starting out, don't get into the trap of thinking that you have to bring in *all* the following elements or that a super complicated spell is more effective than a simple one. What follows are simply options for you to experiment with, try, and explore.

I'll be giving you the instructions for all the ways that you can add energy and magic to a candle before you light it. Take the directions from the following chapters and minimize them by taking out steps, or maximize them by doing all the steps—it's up to you.

Dressing a Candle with Oil

When you are ready to add some extra power to your candle spell, you can do so by adding some herbal magic to your spells. Herbs and essential oils are just two of the tools I like to call "magical allies." Anything that we add to our spell work to align it more with our intention—colors, numbers, timings, petition papers and, of course, herbs and essential oils—will help to keep our intention going, even if we worry about the outcome ourselves.

Sometimes we have a clear intention about what we want when we go into doing our spell, e.g., "I am healthy" or "I have a beautiful new love in my life." We may come out of the gate with that strong positive intention, but then our ego or sometimes even well-meaning friends and family come in to spoil the show. "What if your disease is incurable?" "I'm too old to find love" and all kinds of other "helpful" (that is, not helpful at all) commentary comes in that originates from a place of fear.

Holding these back-and-forth intentions keeps us from moving down the quick and easy path to our goals. It's as if you're taking one step forward ("I can have this good thing") and then one step backward ("It's not possible for me to have this good thing"). One of the primary tenets of magic is "as above, so below," which translates to "if you can imagine it, you can manifest it." If your imagination lacks focus, wavers, or is all over the place, it slows down your manifestation just as driving all over town will slow you down getting to your destination.

When we bring in our magical allies like herbs and oils, the difference is like walking into a party on your own where you know no one or walking into the same party with an entourage of friends. Even if you feel worry or a lack of confidence about your intention, your allies will keep the energy going forward and can even give you a boost of confidence in your spiritual work.

Herbs and essential oils make an excellent team you can add to your magical entourage. Plants have energies and vibrations which can support your intentions. From earliest written history, we find records of herbs being used for medicinal and magical purposes. Through trial and error, ancient people discovered which plants were useful for certain magical purposes, and today there are entire books dedicated to the uses of magical herbs and oils. Everyone practicing magic should own at least one of these books as a reference (some good ones appear in the bibliography). For quick reference, there is also a list of some useful and easy-to-find herbs and essential oils and their magical correspondences right here in this book in appendix I.

The first step of working with oils and herbs is to apply oil to the candle. Applying the oil gives you an excellent opportunity for putting your wishes, intentions, and energy into the candle before you light it. After you do that, you can choose to stop there, or you can apply herbs to the candle or sprinkle them around the candle. You can use a spiritual oil crafted by someone else or create your own. If you are purchasing a prepared oil, I recommend that you use an oil that is more than just a fragrance. Make sure that it has some essential oils in it. How can you tell the difference? Buy from a reputable dealer who lists at least some of the essential oils used in their recipe. Often these high-quality oils can be more expensive than ones made with cheap fragrances, so the price can sometimes (though not always) be a good indicator of quality. Also, if you can see pieces of actual herbs, roots, or flowers in the bottle and the oil has a fragrance, it's a good bet that it also has essential oils in the blend.

Artificial fragrances are not *un*magical—they won't work against your magic. In general, *anything* can be imbued and imprinted with your intention. What essential oils and herbs (and gemstones, shells, and any other natural item) bring to your magic is the helpful spirit of the natural thing. You can take an artificial patchouli fragrance and imbue it with the intention of love, but using the real stuff adds the benefit of patchouli's power to attract a deeply passionate love. Think of fragrances as being like robots that you can program and natural artifacts as being living things that have a helpful spirit and personality all their own.

Whenever working with essential oils, you should dilute them before using them on your skin or a candle. Some essential oils are flammable, and most are irritating to the skin in their undiluted form. Dilute essential oils with a carrier oil such as sweet almond oil, jojoba oil, or apricot kernel oil in a ratio of about ten parts carrier oil per one part (or less) essential oil. A little goes a long way.

There is a lot of fun in creating your own essential oil blend, and doing so is another way to personalize your magic. By making your own oil blend, you can be sure of what's in it and the quality of the products, plus you get to put your own intentions into it as you create it. For your first spiritual oil, I recommend keeping it simple: use only one or two essential oils and a couple of dried herbs. As you become more experienced, you can experiment with creating more complex blends.

Even if you are making a very simple oil with just a few ingredients, always write down your recipes exactly as you create them. A grimoire or personal spell book that contains your recipes for future reference is the perfect place to store this information (see chapter 14 for details on how to record your spells in a grimoire). There's nothing more frustrating than making a beautiful oil that absolutely crushes your magical goals, and then being unable to replicate it because you've forgotten what you put in it.

Recipe for a Basic Spiritual Oil

YOU WILL NEED

Essential oils with droppers or dropper tops

Carrier oil such as sweet almond oil, jojoba oil, apricot kernel oil

Vitamin E oil

Additional dried herbs, roots, and flowers

Dark colored one-ounce bottle for blending and dispensing your oil

Grimoire for recording your recipe

1. Determine what kind of spell your oil will be used for (love, money, protection, etc.) and gather herbs and essential oils that support that spell work. Add a few pinches of dried herbs to your small bottle.

2. Next, add a few drops of your essential oil. You can add up to 10 percent (about one-tenth of the bottle before it's filled) or even just a few drops. Less essential oil does not mean less power.

3. Add a drop of vitamin E oil to prevent the other oils from going rancid.

4. Add the carrier oil and fill to the top.

5. Cap and shake your oil to blend. As you're shaking, you can speak the words of what you want the oil to accomplish magically. I like to do this as an affirmation or a chant.

6. As your oil ages over the next several weeks, it will start to macerate (blend) and smell more complex and harmonious.

Whether you are using an oil prepared by someone else or have created your own, you now have a tool that can add power and nuance to your spell work. Applying an oil to a candle is called "dressing" it, and it is a simple act that infuses your spell with more support, focus, and direction.

You may see some variations on how to apply the oil to a candle. Some say dress it from the center going to the ends, others say hold the candle horizontally with the wick pointing away from you and dress it by pulling the oil toward you for things that you want to bring in and away from you for things you want to banish. These are all fine and valid ways of dressing a candle, but the way I teach it is to hold the candle vertically and apply the oil upward from base to the wick for things you want to bring in, and downward from wick toward the base for things that you want to clear out. Try different methods of dressing, note them in your grimoire, and stick with the method that produces the strongest results and intuitively feels right to you.

As you apply the oil, hold the candle in your hands and feel your energy going into it. Visualize your good outcome and speak words of what you would like the spell to accomplish. Now is the perfect time to charge your candle with all your wishes, intentions, and energy. A candle only needs to be dressed once—before lighting it for the first time. You do not need to dress your candle or add oil every day; in fact, adding more oil can create smoke or other problems.

Once you have dressed your candle, you may apply the remaining oil on your palms to your body in the same way you applied it to the candle: in an upward direction (from feet toward head, fingertips toward shoulders) for drawing something to you and in a downward direction (from head toward feet, shoulders toward fingertips) for driving something away from you.

Candle Spell with Oil

YOU WILL NEED

Freestanding candle

Tray, dish, or candle holder

Prepared spiritual oil

Matches or lighter

1. Pour several drops of spiritual oil into one of your hands.

2. Rub your hands together as you focus on the intention of your spell.

3. Holding the candle in front of you, visualize your good outcome and apply the oil to the sides of the candle as you speak your intention out loud.

4. Set the candle in the holder or affix it to a tray or dish.

5. If you're setting your candle on a tray or dish, heat the wax on the base of the candle with a match. Press it onto the tray so it will stay upright and not fall over.

6. Speak your spell words out loud again as you light the candle.

7. If the oil that you used was to create something positive for yourself, either bringing in something wanted or banishing something unwanted, you can add an extra link to your spell by applying the remaining oil to your skin.

8. Burn the candle while you are at home and awake. If you leave the house or go to sleep, snuff the candle out and relight it when you are able to keep an eye on it.

9. If your candle burns for more than one day, you may optionally apply a few drops of the oil to your body on those days. You can do this before or after you light your candle to make it a mini ritual.

Dressing a Candle with Herbs

Once you have mastered dressing a candle with oil, you are ready to add additional herbs to the mix. Each one of these elements adds nuance and customization to your spell. If you are doing a spell for love, you could start with a sensual patchouli oil, and if you also wanted to bring in an element of commitment and true love, you could add red rose petals to the mix. Adding these herbs gives your spell more depth and supports getting the exact result you want.

There are a few ways you can add the energy of additional herbs to your spell: creating an oil blend (blending patchouli oil and rose oil, for example), adding herbs to your oils (creating a patchouli oil with rose petals in the oil bottle), dressing the candle with oil and sprinkling herbs around the candle (dressing the candle with a patchouli oil blend and sprinkling rose petals around the candle), or dressing the candle with oil and sprinkling dried herbs on the sides or the top of the candle (patchouli oil on the candle and crumbled rose petals on the top or side of the candle).

There are a few special things to note here: woody, fibrous roots, bark, and herbs that are heavy and chunky are best used either as additions to an oil or sprinkled around a candle. Oils are sticky enough for powdered herbs and crumbled leafy herbs and petals to adhere to a candle, but they are not sticky enough for heavy, chunky chopped roots, bark, and woody bits to stick. The law of gravity must be obeyed.

In addition, a little goes a long way. Remember that herbs are flammable. A tiny pinch of an herb is all you need for magic; it will be economical and most importantly, won't catch fire as easily.

There's one final important note about working with herbs and oils. There are more than 300,000 species of plants in the world, of which only a handful have been documented in magical books. However, *all* plants are magical. If you find that you would like to engage with herbs directly, try spending time in nature or in a garden. Connect with the plants and trees around you. Look at a field guide and identify them. Look at the plant itself. Touch and smell it (unless it is poisonous!). Spend time with plants and trees and listen to what they have to teach you. You may attune to new and yet-undiscovered magical purposes for the plants that are right in your backyard.

Candle Spell with Oil and Herbs

YOU WILL NEED

    Freestanding candle

    Tray, dish, or candle holder

Prepared spiritual oil

Powdered herb or light herbs

Chunky, woody herbs

Matches or lighter

1. Pour several drops of spiritual oil into one of your hands.

2. Rub your hands together as you focus on the intention of your spell.

3. Holding the candle upright in front of you, visualize your good outcome, and apply the oil to the sides of the candle as you speak your intention out loud.

4. If the oil that you used was to create something positive for yourself, either bringing in something wanted or banishing something unwanted, you can add an extra link to your spell by applying the remaining oil on your hands to your skin.

5. Sprinkle the powdered or leafy herbs on the side or the top of the candle as you state your spell words or intention.

6. Set the candle in the holder or affix it to a tray or dish.

7. Sprinkle the chunky, heavier herbs around the base of the candle, speaking your spell words out loud as you do.

8. Speak your wish or intention out loud a third time as you light the candle.

9. Burn the candle while you are at home and awake. If you leave the house or go to sleep, snuff the candle out and relight it when you are able to keep an eye on it.

10. If your candle burns for more than one day, you may optionally apply a few drops of the oil to your body on those days. You can do this before or after you light your candle to make it a mini ritual.

Inscribing and Decorating Candles

Inscribing candles is another way to add some extra energy to your spell. Wax is a soft material, so it isn't very difficult to carve power words or symbols into the side of a pillar candle, on the base or side of a figural candle, or on top of a glass-encased vigil to personalize and empower your magic.

Anything with a point can be a tool for inscribing. In a pinch, I have even used an old ballpoint pen or a blunt pencil for inscribing. However, there are lots of other options and some tools that are better than others for inscription. Using a dedicated magical inscribing tool for your candles will imbue them with that little extra bit of power. Nails are also a handy alternative; you can choose a metal that corresponds to your intention. For example, golden-colored brass nails can be used for prosperity and healing; copper nails for love work and the transference of energy; iron for grounding, protection and manifestation; and nickel for problem solving, justice, and empowerment. If you like working with spirits who have passed on, then a forged iron "coffin nail" can be used for calling in assistance from the spirit realm.

When inscribing words into a candle, it is best to be focused and to the point—think key words and brief affirmations. Save your longer phrases and stories for your spoken words or petition paper.

Inscribe Words Horizontally Across the Candle

Holding the candle vertically and inscribing horizontally brings stability, equilibrium and balance to a spell and makes a bold statement. Use horizontal writing when your spell is for calming energy, maintaining the status quo, and holding on to what you already have. When you are connecting a human figural candle to a particular person for sympathetic magic, inscribing their name horizontally across the base (right beneath their feet) connects that candle to the individual. Some people like to write the person's full legal name, others like to write the first name or nickname. In my experience, either method works to energetically connect the candle to the person, because the spell caster ultimately knows who the target is. If you don't know who your target is, e.g., a future lover you haven't yet met or an unknown enemy, you can still inscribe something that indicates them such as "My True Love" or "My Enemies."

Inscribe Words Vertically Across a Candle

Inscribing a candle vertically emphasizes movement and change. It is perfect for straightforward spells that work on the material level where you want immediate results. Inscribe going straight up from base to wick for something you want to bring in or straight down from wick to base for something that you want to clear out or get rid of.

Inscribe Words Around a Candle

Inscribe around the candle in a spiral, like the stripes on a candy cane. Spiraling around the candle is good for complex spells, spiritual intentions, things that have to "gel" correctly, or work that requires the coordination of a lot of moving parts. Wind the words around the candle going up from the base toward the wick for something you want to bring in or going down from the wick toward the base for something you want to clear out.

Inscribe Words Backwards

Writing backward, also called "mirror writing," is used in reversing spells to send negativity back to its source. In this form of writing, words are written backwards but appear forward when held up to a mirror. It is a little more difficult than it sounds. Before you inscribe on your candle,

Inscribed Pillar Candles

I recommend practicing writing your spell words backwards on a piece of paper and then holding the paper up to a mirror to see if anything needs to be fixed. Once you've written it correctly on the paper, use that paper guide and copy the letters on the side of your candle. Generally, you will want to inscribe your mirror writing going down from the wick to the base in a straight line or a spiral, to remove negativity.

Inscribe Symbols Using a Linoleum Block Print Gouge

Nails and inscribers make fine lines that are appropriate for carving words into wax, but if you'd like to carve a deeper, thicker line for a symbol or sigil, linoleum block cutting tools work wonderfully. I recommend using the Speedball U and V gouges as they are safer than the old-fashioned linoleum knives, so you'll be less likely to cut yourself. U and V gouges are called this because when looked at head on, the blade is either U-shaped, which cuts a rounded trough, or V-shaped, which cuts a deep trough with straight sides.

You can also use the gouge end of a candle tool to make these deeper and wider cuts. Dress the cuts with oils and then rub glitter or herbs into the cuts so that your symbols and sigils are beautifully decorated and highlighted against the candle.

Beeswax Appliqué Symbols

Another really lovely way to decorate and add symbolic energy to your candle before you start your spell is to add wax symbols to the surface of the candle. You can use a piece of beeswax in a different color than your candle so that the symbol stands out. Soften the wax with the warmth of your hands or a hair dryer set on warm and mold into symbolic shapes. Press the warmed wax shape onto the side of your candle.

There are a few methods for forming shapes. You can mold a simple shape, such as a heart, from the wax as you're kneading it. You can also roll the wax into long thin "worms" and press them into the sides of the candle to create outlines or write words. You can also melt, press, or roll the wax into thin sheets and use a knife or small cookie cutter to cut out solid shapes such as hearts or stars and gently press them into the wax on your pillar candle to add some extra symbolic magic. For the truly crafty, it's possible to make three-dimensional sculptural elements out of wax such as roses, puffy hearts, tiny skulls, or whatever your spell requires. Simply soften the wax, mold the mini sculpture, and then gently press it onto the surface of the candle. If you need help affixing it, use a hair dryer set on low to warm a small piece of beeswax to stick between your candle and the appliqué.

Whatever method you decide to use, think about choosing colors that add extra subtle elements to your spell. For example, you could prepare a pink candle for a heart-centered, romantic love and apply red hearts to the sides to add an element of passion and sizzle to the relationship. Want to add even more to your symbol? Blend a pinch of powdered herbs into the wax as you are softening it to add the energy and power of that herb.

Loading a Candle

Loading a candle is a technique for preparing a candle with herbs, petition papers, or personal concerns (such as a piece of hair or a fingernail clipping) while keeping the magical work secret. Instead of putting herbs on the outside, they are placed inside. Putting your magical support items inside makes your candle appear to be a basic decorative object to the casual observer while secretly it is infused with the items' energy.

CUSTOMIZING YOUR SPELL CANDLES

Sometimes it makes sense to take the extra effort to prepare a candle this way. If you are trying to keep your magical work hidden from others, a loaded candle will keep your work on the down-low. If you are moving a candle to another location, loading your candle will prevent herbs from falling off the tray or getting knocked off the outside of the candle. If you are gifting a prepared candle to another person and don't want them to know that the candle has been prepared, loading a candle and then putting it in a holder or glass jar can keep your work from being discovered.

If you'd like to load a candle, first choose a freestanding candle wide enough that you can carve a hole in it at least the size of the tip of your thumb. Taper candles are too slender and will break; a wide pillar candle or figural candle with a wide base is ideal.

 Loaded Candle Spell

YOU WILL NEED

Wide, freestanding candle

Small pieces of herbs

Tray or dish

Sharp paring knife

Hair dryer

Lighter or matches

Small gemstone chips (optional)

Small petition paper (optional)

Small curios (optional)

Personal concerns (optional) (For more on personal concerns, see the section on Honey Jars in chapter 10)

1. Before you begin, gather the items that you are going to load inside the candle. Less is more. Small amounts of herbs and other items are all that you need. In total, your items should take up a space no larger than the tip of your thumb.

2. With the knife (or a candle tool), carve a hole in the bottom of the candle. Reserve the wax that you carve out.

3. Place herbs and any other curios inside the hole.

4. Cover the herbs with the remaining wax chips that you had removed, pressing the wax and herbs into the hole firmly. The wax should cover the herbs completely and should extend slightly beyond the level of the base of the candle.

5. Light your match or lighter or use a hair dryer set to high heat. Heat the wax and press the softened wax with the side of your knife to seal in the herbs. Flatten the wax until it is flush with the base, making the hole undetectable.

6. While holding the candle in your hands, visualize your intentions, put your energy into the candle, and speak your spell words.

7. Speak your spell words out loud again as you light the candle.

8. Burn the candle while you are at home and awake. If you leave the house or go to sleep, snuff the candle out and relight it when you are able to keep an eye on it.

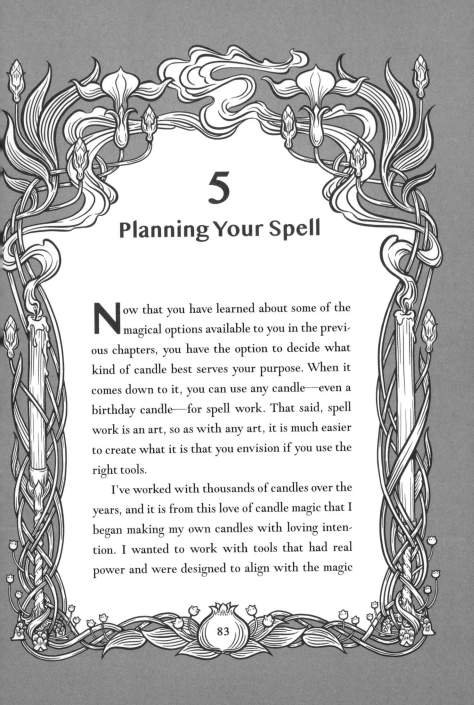

5

Planning Your Spell

Now that you have learned about some of the magical options available to you in the previous chapters, you have the option to decide what kind of candle best serves your purpose. When it comes down to it, you can use any candle—even a birthday candle—for spell work. That said, spell work is an art, so as with any art, it is much easier to create what it is that you envision if you use the right tools.

I've worked with thousands of candles over the years, and it is from this love of candle magic that I began making my own candles with loving intention. I wanted to work with tools that had real power and were designed to align with the magic

I wished to do. I saw the difference in the power of my spells when they were done with a candle that was "witch-made" versus a factory-made candle off the shelf. When you start out with energetically charged tools, you can give your work an amazing boost of power.

I have also been in a pinch, where the only thing available was a bargain basement tea light. While it might not have had the loving energy of a handcrafted candle, I believe it is far better to do a spell with *any* tool than doing no spell at all.

There are many things to consider before choosing a candle for your spell. "What am I doing a spell for?" is just the start. Before starting, I recommend sitting down with a piece of paper, your journal, or your grimoire and mapping out your spell game plan (see chapter 14 for details on creating a grimoire). Spending some time to consider these questions and coming up with thoughtful choices will empower your spell before you even strike a match.

These are some of the questions you may want to consider when choosing a candle for your spell. The first one is required, but the rest are thought-provoking possible directions that you can take your spell work, some of which will be elaborated on in the chapters to come. You don't have to take all of these questions into consideration, but pondering these possibilities will help you design an amazing spell.

- What is the objective of my spell?
- Would I like to do a simple spell where I can just light the candle and go, or would I like to spend time and energy to craft a more complex candle spell that has subtlety and is totally customized to my situation?

- How much do I want to spend on my spell? Would I like to buy the very best materials for my spell or choose lower-cost items to stay within a certain budget?

- Do I want to choose a specific color candle to support my spell work?

- Do I want a candle that is infused with oils and/or herbs or do I want a plain candle that I have the option of dressing with oil and herbs myself?

- Do I want a candle that is shaped symbolically to support my spell work?

- Do I want a candle with fragrance or do I want a fragrance-free candle?

- Do I want a candle that comes in a glass container or do I want a freestanding candle that I put in a candle holder or affix to a tray?

- Do I want to make my own candle, work with a candle made by someone who has put magical intention into it, or will one made by machines in a factory serve my needs?

- Would I like to purchase a spell kit that gives me step-by-step instructions and all the materials I need, or do I want to source my spell materials myself?

- How much time do I have to do the spell? Is it for something I need right this minute or do I have some time to start a spell on the perfect date and hour and work it over many days?

Before diving into the chapters to come, these questions might seem overwhelming. I promise that by the time you've finished this book, they will seem empowering. While there are no right or wrong answers, it's best to think about your needs, constraints, and personal preferences before starting a candle spell. Spending time in contemplation is excellent magical preparation and will help you choose a candle and other tools that will bring the strongest alignment to your spell.

Once you've determined what candle you want to use, think about the other elements you want to bring in: colors, numbers, herbs, and so on. How can you keep all those moving pieces in mind when just starting out? Remember that you don't have to incorporate *all* the elements covered in this book into a single candle spell. Even experienced practitioners use just a handful of elements in their workings. Adding too much will drive you batty.

To get your focus and know what you want to bring in, make a list of three of the most important objectives of your spell after you have done your free-writing and written your petition. If you're thinking of more than three, you probably need to do more than one spell. Once you list those things, think of the creative way to incorporate that energy into your spell work through the elements available.

Reconciliation Spell Plan Example

Petition: John Smith and I are back together

> **OBJECTIVE 1:** I want him to forget about the argument we had.
>
> **OBJECTIVE 2:** I want our relationship to be strong and solid.
>
> **OBJECTIVE 3:** I want the romance in our relationship to come back.

There are a lot of options for addressing these issues in your candle spell but here's an example:

> **OBJECTIVE 1:** I want him to forget about the argument we had. I'm going to sprinkle poppy seeds around the candle so that he forgets about the argument.

OBJECTIVE 2: I want our relationship to be strong and solid. I'm going to use four candles because the number four represents strength and stability.

OBJECTIVE 3: I want the romance in our relationship to come back. I'm going to use pink candles so that his heart-centered emotions return.

You see how when you break it down, it's easy to incorporate multiple elements for the subtle nuances of your objectives.

When Do I Light My Spell Candle?

My belief is that if you need a spell right now, then do your candle spell right away. But if you can wait a few days to work with a time that aligns best with your intention, you'll be able to harness an extra boost of energy to add to your spell. Think of it as the difference between pushing a cart on a flat surface versus downhill. When you harness timing that supports your intention, the pushing becomes much easier.

There are a few choices in regard to timing your candle spell.

Working with Holidays or Special Days

Whether secular or religious, holidays are a great time to do a candle spell. Doing a blessing spell on a birthday, a love spell on Valentine's Day, or a prosperity spell on New Year's Day are all examples of harnessing communal energy to empower a spell. These kinds of spells tend to be ones based on awareness of the holiday coming up. Secular or religious holidays, anniversaries, birthdays, holy days, solstices, and equinoxes are all days that have a certain energy to them. You can harness this energy by looking at what the day represents and using that energy to empower your spells. For example, you could use the upcoming birthday of a celebrity to harness their energy for a fame spell for yourself or a wedding anniversary for a spell to bless your own relationship.

Working with Moon Phases

There are two basic lunar phases that can be harnessed for candle magic:

Waning Moon

This is the time when the moon appears to grow smaller, from the full moon to the new or dark moon. The waning moon is the time to do spell work about clearing, removing and banishing; for example, clearing out negativity and removing unhealthy patterns.

Waxing Moon

This is the time when the moon appears to be growing larger, from the new or dark moon to the full moon. The waxing phase is the time to do spell work about invocation, attraction and bringing in; for example, attracting a lover or bringing in more abundance.

Some candle spell intentions work at maximum effectiveness during the waning moon (such as spells for purification or to reverse negativity). Others work best during a waxing moon (such as attraction or prosperity spells). However, some spells can be done at any moon phase (tranquility spells, for example, can be charged to release arguments or invite in peace). If possible, try to time beginning your candle with the early part of the moon phase so that you can burn it completely before the phase is complete.

There is a really lovely way to create some powerful magic by accessing the power of both the waning *and* the waxing moon. First, do a candle spell to clear out the negative blocks during the waning moon, clearing the way for something new, and then follow it up with a drawing or attraction candle spell to invite in what you want during the waxing moon.

Here are some examples:

WANING MOON: Removing poverty mindset

WAXING MOON: Creating abundance

WANING MOON: Banishing self-limiting beliefs

WAXING MOON: Inviting success

WANING MOON: Clearing out old relationship baggage

WAXING MOON: Attracting a soulmate into your life

Dark Moon and Full Moon

Witches and other moon-centered folks like to harness two other special moon phase timings—the full moon and the dark moon. These phases traditionally take place on the three days before and after the night of the event. You'll find lots of differing opinions on what kind of magic to do on these special days of the month, but I was taught to work them in the following way.

Dark Moon

The night of the dark moon (sometimes called the new moon) is the time right before the moon is waxing, so you complete your waning moon magic and you "plant the seeds" of the things that you want to grow. Do your quiet, internal, solitary work during this time and work on activating new beginnings.

Full Moon

The night of the full moon is the culmination of the waxing moon and the time right before the moon is waning, so you celebrate the success of your waxing moon magic and you start the releasing process again. Do group work and joyful magic with others during this time. It is also a powerful time for dream work and psychic work.

Working with Astrological Phenomena

Astrology is a fascinating topic to explore and you can use even a basic understanding to coordinate your candle work.

Working with the Moon Astrologically

Astrologically speaking, the moon is the planet of magic, mysteries, psychic phenomena, and deep emotion. Unlike some of the more distant planets, it goes through a new sign every couple of days, so it's easier to coordinate an auspicious timing. There are many websites and apps with calendars that can tell you what sign the moon is in so that you can coordinate your ideal timing.

Feel the different energy as the Moon moves through the zodiac. Think about the spell work you might want to coordinate when the moon (or another planet) is in the following signs:

Aries ♈

Physical strength, war, victory, beginnings, will, force, fearlessness, new ventures, resilience.

Taurus ♉

Prosperity, work, sensuality, pleasure, perseverance, longevity in love, business, security, luxury.

Gemini ♊

Multi-tasking, twin flames, mental pursuits, communication, wit, creativity, socializing, partnership.

Cancer ♋

Home, parenting, sustenance, domesticity, intuition, change, marriage, artistry, family, children, divination.

Leo ♌

Fame, recognition, leadership, courage, power, victory, success, confidence, self-esteem.

Virgo ♍

Details, service to others, organization, order, safety, writing, help, truth, healing, problem solving.

Libra ♎

Balance, harmony, beauty, justice, diplomacy, peace, compatibility, cooperation.

Scorpio ♏

Endings, sex, processing grief and death, loyalty, revenge, passion, control, competition, mystery.

Sagittarius ♐

Adventure, travel, philosophy, freedom, opening opportunities, risk, luck.

Capricorn ♑

Business, long-range plans, empire-building, tradition, learning, structure, stability, abundance, success.

Aquarius ♒

Innovation, ground-breaking ideas, technology, originality, trailblazing, pushing boundaries.

Pisces ♓

Psychic awareness, dream work, emotions, creativity, mysticism, spirituality, endings, empathy.

Working with Planets

As you become more familiar with astrology, you might want to coordinate your candle around the sun or the planets being in certain signs to enhance your work. For example, you might want to do a marriage spell when Venus is in the sign of Cancer, a spell for professional success as a performer when the Sun is in Leo, or enemy work when Mars is in Aries.

You can also coordinate so that you work with the planets when they are in their exalted signs, that is, the signs where the power of the planet is at its peak.

Sun—Aries

Moon—Taurus

Mars—Capricorn

Mercury—Virgo

Jupiter—Cancer

Venus—Pisces

Saturn—Libra

Working with Days of the Week

Some practitioners use days of the week to coordinate when to light candles. There are days of the week that give a boost to working with certain kinds of magic and starting your spell on these days can give a burst of power to your spells.

Each day of the week has one of the seven ancient "planets" associated with it. You can use this correspondence to coordinate working the planetary energies into your spell work too by inscribing the symbol of the planet onto your candle.

Sunday (Sun) ☉

Outward energy, authority, leadership, healing, blessing, general positive work, optimism, advancement, fame, recognition, success, will, beauty.

Monday (Moon) ☽

Internal energy, dream work, psychic work, emotions, spirituality, marriage, inspiration, intuition, secrets, personal or internal work, childbirth, fertility, family, home.

Tuesday (Mars) ♂

Aggression, courage, hunting, vitality, strategizing, conflict, break ups, banishing, destruction, strength, vigorous health, victory, competition.

Wednesday (Mercury) ☿

Communication, business transactions, travel, negotiations, faster results, gambling, creativity, intelligence, resourcefulness, speaking, writing, messages, trickster energy.

Thursday (Jupiter) ♃

Power, wealth, success, leadership, money, business building, legal issues, expansion, justice, politics, loyalty, attracting clients, regal bearing.

Friday (Venus) ♀

Love, lust, sex, beauty, harmony, prosperity, admiration, creativity, attraction, friendship, pleasure, art, music, partnerships, seduction, aesthetics, money.

Saturday (Saturn) ♄

Motivation, will, clarifying, creating structure, enemy work, binding, blocking, revenge, knowledge, tradition, duty, limitation, boundaries.

Working with Day and Night

In addition to working with a certain day for magic, you can also harness the energy of the time of day. One simple form of working with the time of day is to start your candle spell at sunrise, noon, sunset, or midnight.

Sunrise

Start candles for new endeavors, fresh new beginnings, building energy, increase and the attraction of good things at dawn.

Noon

Start candles for success, power, abundance, wealth, stability and strength at noon.

Sunset

Sunset is the perfect time for banishing, releasing, break up, separation, endings, cord-cutting, or cleansing magic.

Midnight

Considered the "witching hour," midnight is a powerful time to do spells for psychic abilities, spirit contact, shadow work, hidden or secret work, mental influence, supernatural work, and working in otherworldly or alternate realities.

Working with the Time of the Day

Another simple way to work with the time of day is to focus on the hours of the day. This system works especially well with digital clocks. Simply start your spell at a time with a repeating number (for example, 3:33, 9:09, or 20:20). Choose a number that corresponds to the intention of your spell (see chapter 8 for a breakdown on numerology). You can do this using both the 12-hour and 24-hour clock systems; if using a 12-hour clock, choose an a.m. time for spells of increase and a p.m. time for spells of release.

Another old-fashioned way to work with the time of day is to use an old-school analog clock and use times when the hour and minute hands are "rising" (moving from 6 to 12) for increase and using times when the hands are "falling" (moving from 12 to 6) for clearing out something unwanted. For example, at the time of 7:35 (a.m. or p.m.) both hands would be rising up the left side of the clock, so this would be an excellent time for attraction work, while at 2:18 both hands would be moving down the right side of the clock so this would be a good time to cleanse away something negative.

Working with Planetary Hours

Another magical way to work with the time of day and also work with astrology was developed in ancient Greece—the planetary hours. According to this system, each day is divided into twelve equal parts between sunrise and sunset and also into twelve equal parts between sunset and sunrise. Each of these segments has a planet attached to it and working during that time can give your spell a boost of the energy of that planet. There are ways to mathematically find the planetary hours, but it's much simpler these days to just find a planetary hours calculator online or download an app. Start your spell work during the planetary hour that most supports your spell.

Hour of the Sun

Health, job, career, promotion, leadership, performance, fame, presentations, social status, authority figures.

Hour of the Moon

Change, cycles, intuition, psychic work, creative imagination, dream work, home, family, marriage.

Hour of Mercury

Mental alertness, communication, business transactions, travel, negotiations, technology, gambling, mental creativity, intelligence, resourcefulness, speaking, writing, messages, trickster energy.

Hour of Venus

Love, courtship, marriage, lust, beauty, sex, harmony, prosperity, admiration, aesthetic creativity, sociability, attraction, friendship, pleasure, art, music, partnerships, seduction, aesthetics, peace, calm, mediation, money matters.

Hour of Mars

Aggression, exertion, courage, hunting, vitality, strategizing, conflict, break ups, banishing, destruction, strength, boldness, vigorous health, victory, competition.

Hour of Jupiter

Politics, power, wealth, attracting followers, success, leadership, money, business building, legal issues, expansion, justice, loyalty.

Hour of Saturn

Organization, motivation, will, clarifying, breaking bad habits, creating structure, responsibility, enemy work, binding, blocking, revenge, knowledge, tradition, duty, limitation, boundaries.

6

Making Magic Candles

While it is a common idea that candles used for magic must be handmade, most spell casters do their magic with commercially made candles and there is absolutely nothing wrong with that. Your spell tools are vessels that carry *your* energy. However, as you start doing more candle magic, you will naturally become more conscious about the products used in your work. Purchasing candles handmade by people who imbue their products with love and care as they make them will have a positive effect on your work ... and purchasing candles specifically made for magic by magic practitioners, even more so.

As you become more adept at candle magic, it's useful to understand everything that goes into the candlemaker's craft. One of the things I love to teach my students is how to make their own candles. Again, it's not that you *need* to make every candle you use in every spell, but it's useful in a practical way to understand how candles are made, and on a spiritual level, making a candle from scratch gives you an opportunity to add even more power and intention to your spell.

In the following sections, I share my secrets for magical candle crafting: how to make candles that are charged with your spell's intention for your extra special spells.

Rolled Beeswax Candles

Rolled beeswax candles are some of the easiest candles to create; you don't need to melt wax or have any special equipment to make a beautiful and customized taper candle for your spell. Like a plain taper candle, you can add spiritual oils and small amounts of herbs to the candle, but instead of just applying them to the outside, you can add them as you roll the beeswax to integrate them all throughout the candle.

You can purchase thin sheets of beeswax that are pressed into a honeycomb pattern, called beeswax foundation, and roll them around a primed wick to create a taper candle. Primed wick is a candle wick that has already been dipped in wax to make it rigid and easier to roll (and easier to light once the candle is made). If you can't get primed wick, raw wick (just plain cotton wick with no wax) can also be used. You can also prime raw wick yourself by dipping it in melted beeswax and letting it harden before you get started.

Making a Rolled Beeswax Candle

YOU WILL NEED

Sheet of beeswax foundation

Square braided cotton wick size 2/0 or 3/0 (not to be confused with #2 or #3 which are for much bigger candles). The length of the wick should be about ½" (12 mm) longer than your beeswax foundation.

Spiritual oil

Pinch of dried herbs

1. Lay the sheet of beeswax foundation on a table. Choose wax in a color that corresponds to your spell work.

2. Apply a few drops of an appropriate spiritual oil over the top side of your beeswax staying about 1" (24 mm) from the edges.

3. Sprinkle a small pinch of dried herbs over the top side of the beeswax. CAUTION: Dried herbs, flowers, and roots are flammable. In most cases, a small amount will not cause a problem, but if you get overly enthusiastic with your herb application, you'll have a candle that can catch fire all over. More herbs (or oils, candles, or *anything* for that matter) *do not* equal more power in your spell.

4. Place the wick across one end of the foundation with the extra wick hanging over on one side.

5. Roll the wax around the wick. If you are making a candle to clear away something, you can start with the wick close to you and roll the candle away from you. If you are making a candle to bring

something to you, you can start with the wick on the edge of the wax that is farthest from you and roll the candle toward you.

6. As you are rolling the candle, chant your spell words to bless the candle for your specific intention.

7. Once you've rolled the wax completely around the candle, gently press down the edge into the candle so that it makes a seam and holds the candle together.

8. The side with the extra wick is the top of your candle. Trim it down to ¼" (6 mm) and it's ready to light for your spell.

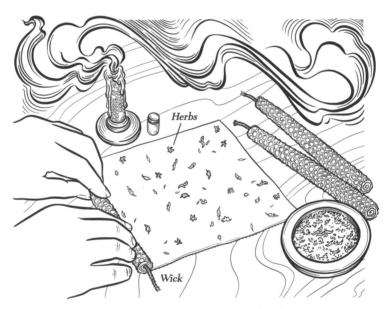

Herbs

Wick

How to Make a Rolled Beeswax Candle

EXTRA TIP: Experiment by rolling sheets of beeswax that are different heights and widths to make tall slim candles or short wide ones. You can roll a sheet of beeswax cut into a right triangle to make a tapered cone-shaped candle that is tall in the center with sloping sides.

Dipped Taper Candles

Dipped tapers are quite involved but worth the effort if you want to make a magical candle from scratch. Before the introduction of candle molds, all tapers were made by being dipped. If you've ever been to an old-time crafts fair or historical reenactment site, you may have even had the opportunity to do this activity yourself. The process of dipping a taper candle is to take a piece of raw or primed wick and dip it into a vat of melted wax. Each time you dip it in, a layer is built on the wick. Do it over and over again, and enough layers are built up to create a taper candle.

One of the beautiful aspects of dipped candles is that you can say your spell words each time you dip the wick into the pot of melted wax, making a deeply magical candle.

Making a Dipped Taper Candle

YOU WILL NEED

1 lb/.5 kg beeswax (2 lbs/1 kg if you are going to make a longer candle)

Primed square braided cotton wick size 2/0 or 3/0 (not to be confused with #2 or #3, which are for much bigger candles). The length of the wick needs to be about double the length of your finished candle.

Large, clean can (a 46 oz/1300 ml tomato juice can is about right)

Old cooking pot large enough to hold the juice can (you *will* get wax on it and, while beeswax is nontoxic, it's a pain to clean up, so don't use your good cookware).

Cooking thermometer (candy thermometer or meat thermometer that measures to 155°F/68°C)

Scissors or knife

Candle dye (optional)

Lid to a cooking pot (optional). You may want to have this on hand, just in case you need to snuff out a fire.

1. Put beeswax in your clean juice can.

2. Create a double boiler by placing the juice can in the cooking pot and filling the pot ½ to ¾ with water. Don't add water to the wax can, just to the pot.

3. Heat on a low flame. Heat the water to lower than a simmer, and never boiling. Wax is flammable and if you heat it too hot, it could catch fire.

4. Be patient! Depending on the amount of beeswax you are melting and whether it is in small pieces or one large chunk, it can take three or more hours for the wax to melt.

5. Check the temperature of the water at intervals and make sure it is about 150° to 155°F/68°C. Lower than 150°F/65°C, your wax won't be melted enough and you'll end up with a lumpy candle (if you can make one at all). Higher than 160°F/71°C, the wax will be too hot to build layers. At temperatures higher than 185°F/85°C, the wax will be ruined and become a fire hazard.

6. Once the wax is melted, you can add candle dye. Use *only* candle dye. Other coloring, such as crayons, food coloring, cloth dye, etc., will not blend with wax or are not safe for candles.

7. Begin by dipping the wick into the melted wax. After you pull it out, let it cool for a moment and then pull on both ends of the wick to straighten it. Let it cool for about 45 to 60 seconds.

8. There is a technique to dipping candles. Don't leave them dipped in the wax for too long. If you do, you'll heat up the layers of wax that you've built up and melt them off. The trick is to dip the wick in and out quickly and let it harden for about 30 to 60 seconds before dipping it in again.

9. As you make each dip, say your spell words to infuse your candle with powerful intention.

10. As you dip, wax will build up like an icicle at the bottom of your taper. Trim this off with scissors or a knife from time to time as you are dipping or right before you do your final few dips. The trimmed wax can go back in the melting pot.

11. When the candle is about as thick as your finger, you're done. Let it harden completely overnight. If you want to add some extra magic, let it harden somewhere where it can pick up the light of the moon.

12. Trim the wick down to about ¼" (6 mm). Your magical candle is ready for lighting.

Dipping of Candles

If you decide to work with another kind of wax other than beeswax, please do your research. Different waxes have different melting points and need different types of wick.

Herb-Rolled Taper Candles

Herb-rolled candles are a variation on dipped candles. By adding herbs to the outside of your taper, you can add the power of the herbs to assist with your spell. They also look very rustic and witchy and are fun to work with if you like your spell candles to look extra magical. Two variations on this follow. The first method is for after dipping a candle from scratch. The second method doesn't require candle dipping equipment.

Making an Herb-Rolled
Taper Candle–Dipped Method

YOU WILL NEED

Beeswax taper candle

Beeswax dipped taper tools (can of beeswax in pot of water)

Cookie sheet or flat tray

Dried herbs that support your spell's intention

Tongs, clothespin, or clip

1. Prepare wax for dipped tapers as described in the recipe above.

2. Sprinkle light and crumbly herbs on a cookie sheet.

3. Bless the herbs by holding your hands over them and visualizing your magical goal.

4. Dip a regular beeswax taper candle (a purchased candle or one you have made) in the hot wax two or three times, waiting 30 to 45 seconds between each dip. If you are using a purchased candle with a short wick, you will need to use tongs, a clothespin, or a clip so that you can dip the candle in the hot wax and keep your fingers safe.

5. As you dip your candles, you can say your spell words to add some extra power to your working.

6. After the last dip, wait just five to ten seconds and then roll your candle back and forth in the herbs on the cookie sheet, pressing the herbs into the warm wax of the candle.

7. As with all herbs and candles, go easy on the extra herbal matter. Herbs are flammable, so you don't want to add too many.

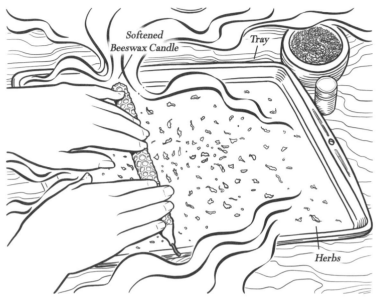

Rolling Candle in Herbs

8. Optional step: Let the candle rest for I to 2 minutes and then dip it one more time in the wax to seal the herbs in place. Note that some of the herbs from your candle may fall off into your wax. They'll probably sink to the bottom of the wax but, if they're light, they may get into your next candle spell. Unless the herbs are powdered, you can always strain your candle wax through a scrap of cheesecloth to clear out any herbs that get mixed in.

9. Let the candle harden completely overnight. If you want to add some extra magic, let it harden somewhere where it can pick up the light of the moon.

10. If this is a candle you have made from scratch, trim the wick down to about ¼" (6 mm). Your magical candle is now ready for lighting.

11. Pay extra close attention to an herb-dipped candle as you are burning it so you can snuff it out if the herbs catch on fire.

12. Snuff your candle out when you go to sleep or leave the house and relight it when you return.

Making an Herb-Rolled Taper Candle–Hair Dryer Method

Rather than dip a candle in wax, you can take a prepared beeswax candle and heat it with a hair dryer set to hot and then roll the candle in the herbs. It's important that it's a beeswax taper, as paraffin tapers will not soften or get sticky enough to let the herbs stick. Use the hair dryer on your candle somewhere far away from your herbs on the tray. You don't want to accidentally blow away all your herbs!

YOU WILL NEED

Beeswax taper candle

Cookie sheet or flat tray

Dried herbs that support your spell's intention

Hair dryer

1. Sprinkle the herbs on the cookie sheet

2. Bless the herbs by holding your hands over them and visualizing your magical goal.

3. Take a regular beeswax taper candle (a purchased candle or one you have made) and blow hot air from a hair dryer over one side of the candle to soften the wax.

4. After one side is soft, immediately roll the soft side of the candle back and forth in the herbs on the cookie sheet, pressing the herbs into the warm wax of the candle.

5. Repeat with the other side of the candle.

6. As with all herbs and candles, just use a little bit. Remember that herbs are flammable—more herbs do not equal more power.

7. If this is a candle that was cooled and hardened before you started, you only need to let the candle set for 10 to 20 minutes.

8. Trim the wick down to about ¼" (6 mm). Your magical candle is now ready for lighting.

9. Pay extra close attention to an herb-dipped candle as you are burning it so you can snuff it out if the herbs catch on fire.

10. Snuff your candle out when you go to sleep or leave the house and relight it when you return.

Fixed Vigil Lights

Vigil candles are the tall beeswax or paraffin pillar candles that are encased in long, slender glass jars. Vigil lights have a special place in candle magic, as they burn extra long and are relatively safe. That longer burn is great for stubborn spiritual matters that need a push. The glass candle jar can also be decorated with stickers, labels, or paint pens.

While it's possible to purchase a fixed vigil light, for your purposes as an experienced candle spell caster you will want to purchase a plain candle without herbs, oils or fragrance, so that you can dress and bless it yourself. The burning of fixed vigil candles is sometimes called "the setting of lights," and this section will tell you how to prepare a fixed vigil light.

Making a Fixed Vigil Light

YOU WILL NEED

Plain, unscented, undressed vigil candle

Dried herbs

Spiritual oil

Dropper for oil

Long, sharp tool such as a screwdriver, awl, icepick, metal chopstick, or metal knitting needle

Prepared petition paper

Glitter (optional)

Paint pens or permanent markers (optional)

1. Choose a candle of a color that supports your intention (see the Candle Color section). You can also choose a candle with a label or silkscreened image that supports your outcome.

2. Holding your candle firmly, poke seven holes in the top of the candle in a circle around the wick with your long, sharp tool. Poke down as far as you can go. With soft soy wax or paraffin, you might be able to poke a hole a few inches deep. With firm beeswax, you may only be able to poke down a few millimeters. As you do, you can repeat your spell words each time. Do this in a clockwise

direction to bring something in, or in a counterclockwise direction to clear something out.

3. Alternatively, you can choose a number other than seven that corresponds to your spell's intention (see chapter 8 for guidance on using numbers to enhance your candle magic).

4. With a dropper, place one drop of spiritual oil in each hole. As you do, you can again speak your spell words. One drop per hole is sufficient. Too much oil will cause a smoky burn and leave soot on the glass that will give a false negative reading to the candle remains.

5. Sprinkle a very small pinch of the herbs that support your work on the top. As you sprinkle your herbs, you can ask them to support your spell's intention. Be sparing with the herbs. Again, if you use too many, they will catch fire when you light your candle and at the very least, create sooty smoke that may give a false negative to your candle reading. Too many herbs on fire can also create extra heat that can crack your candle glass or create a blaze you will have to contend with.

6. If you would like to add some additional color magic, you can sprinkle some glitter in a color that matches your candle color or in an alternate support color.

7. If you'd like to decorate the glass of the candle with words, sigils, symbols, or magical designs, you can do so with a paint pen or permanent marker.

8. Place your petition paper under the candle.

9. Hold one or both of your hands over the top of the candle and pray over your candle or visualize your intention.

10. Light your candle as you speak your petition.

11. Snuff your candle out when you go to sleep or leave the house and relight it when you return.

 Making a Fixed Vigil Light with a Pull-Out

Vigil candle pull-outs can also be prepared like a regular vigil light, but pull-outs have the advantage that you can dress and decorate the outside surface of the wax before you pop it into the glass holder.

YOU WILL NEED

Glass vigil candle holder

Plain vigil candle pull-out

Inscribing tool (candle inscriber, nail, linoleum block gouge, candle tool)

Spiritual oil

Dropper or paint brush

Glitter and/or powdered herbs

Soft cloth for wiping off glitter (an old T-shirt works great for this)

Additional dried herbs that support your spell's intention

Prepared petition paper

Newspaper to protect your table

1. Before starting, you may want to lay down newspaper to collect the carved wax and excess glitter that will fall from your candle.

2. Choose a candle of a color that supports your intention.

3. Using your inscribing or carving tool, you can carve words, sigils, symbols, or designs that support your intention into the side of your candle. Carve these deep and wide enough so that glitter or powdered herbs can get embedded in the grooves.

4. Using a dropper or paint brush, put the spiritual oil into the carved inscriptions.

5. Dust the candle with glitter and/or powdered herbs over the grooves.

6. Don't worry if you don't stay in the lines. Wipe down the excess with a soft rag so that the majority of the herbs/glitter remains just in the grooves.

7. Place your candle in the glass vigil holder.

Pull-Out Candle

8. Sprinkle a very small pinch of the herbs that support your work on the top of the candle. As you sprinkle your herbs, you can ask them to support your spell's intention.

9. If you would like to add some additional color magic, you can sprinkle a small amount of glitter on top of the candle in a color that matches your candle color or in an alternate support color.

10. Place the folded petition paper beneath your candle holder.

11. Hold one or both of your hands over the top of the candle and pray over your candle or visualize your intention.

12. Light your candle as you speak your spell words.

13. Snuff your candle out when you go to sleep or leave the house and relight it when you return.

Series of Vigil Lights

Vigil lights may be done individually or done as a series of two or more lights. If you choose to do a series, you can do them over a certain amount of time or do a certain number of candles. (Check out chapter 8 for more information on numerology and working with multiple candles consecutively.)

Spirit Candles and Altar Candles

Spiritualists, devotees, and people who want the assistance of their ancestors, deities, saints, angels, or spirit guides may want to use a candle to invite a spirit into their presence. These candles are sometimes called altar candles or spirit candles. These candles are not done for a wish or spell but are simply an ongoing way to honor and welcome a spirit or ask for assistance and protection. Usually, a larger candle that can be burned over several days is used for this purpose: a large pillar candle or a vigil candle are typically used.

Choose a color that is associated with the particular spirit, or a white or metallic silver candle, if there is no special color association. Some people choose a glass-encased vigil candle that is decorated with the image of the saint or deity that they are invoking, but if a ready-made version doesn't exist, you can easily make one, either by pasting an image to the glass with white glue, using a computer printer to make a paper sticker, or drawing or painting the name, symbols, or an image of the spirit on the glass using a paint pen.

Dedicate your spirit candle by holding the candle and envisioning the spirit and speaking words to invite them into your presence. You can light the candle during ritual when you invite the spirit to be in your presence or during meditation when you would like to connect with the spirit. Snuff the candle out when you would like to dismiss or release the spirit. Some people like to burn these spirit candles alongside their spell candles so that they get the support of the spirit to help with their intentions.

Another way to work with this kind of candle is to set up a spirit altar (a small altar dedicated to the spirit) and allow the candle to burn continuously whenever you are awake and at home.

Unlike spell candles, spirit candles are not burned with the intention of completion but are burned whenever you would like to invite a connection, communication, or the help of a spirit. When your candle is nearing completion, it is traditional to prepare and dedicate a new candle of the same kind, lighting it with the flame of the old one. You can use a match or a taper candle to transfer the flame from the old candle to the new one. Once the new one is lit, snuff the old candle out and dispose of it.

Secret Spells

Most of the time when we picture spells, we imagine gorgeous spiritual altars covered with candles and radiating power, but not all spells can be done this way. What if you live in a house with people who don't appreciate your fabulous witchiness? What if you want to do a spell on a person but don't want them to know you're doing a spell on them? There are times when we need our magic to say, "These aren't the droids you're looking for." (And just like that, my *Star Wars* nerdery comes out!).

In your magical journey, there may be times when you want your spell to go unnoticed. Whatever your reasons, here are some tips for keeping your spell work hidden in plain sight.

First, choose a candle that doesn't look too "magic-y." Tall tapers and pillar candles are pretty mundane-looking. You can see candles like these on dinner tables, in bedrooms or in bathrooms and no one thinks twice about them. In fact, almost everyone defaults to looking at them as non-magical candles, which can work in your favor. So, choose one of these candles for your candle spell and you can keep it really secret.

If you really, *really* have to be secretive about it, like "no-one-can-ever-see-me-burn-a-candle" secret, you can use a very small candle that will burn quickly and use it while you have some privacy, either by burning the candle when others are out of the house or even going into a locked bathroom to do your spell work. A typical chime candle will burn in less than thirty minutes and a birthday candle will burn in less than five minutes.

To keep things on the down-low and still be magical, you can apply an oil to the candle and no one will be any the wiser. Oils might add a sheen, but most non-magical folks won't notice. There's also no need to sprinkle herbs if you're trying to make your candle work unnoticeable. If you dress your candle in a spiritual oil blend, you are applying the energies of the herbs in a nearly invisible way.

You can also hide your petition paper inside a candle holder or underneath a tray. If you're doing your spell with a taper, you can use a traditional metal candle holder. Write your petition on a tiny paper and place it in the candle holder underneath the candle. If your candle holder has a hollow base, you can stuff your petition paper up inside the base of the candle holder and it will be virtually invisible. For larger pillar candles burned on decorative trays, you can place a very small petition paper underneath the candle, and it should be unnoticeable.

If working with a larger pillar candle, you can load the candle: carve out a small hole in the bottom of the candle, put your petition paper and any herbs inside, and seal up the hole with wax. Check out the Loading a Candle section in chapter 4 for details.

7

The Special Magic of Figural Candles

Figural candles are candles that are representative of something. These are candles molded into the shape of something recognizable; for example a cat, a pair of lips, or a human figure. Figural candles bring in a strong symbolic visual connection that accesses the deepest part of our consciousness.

Symbolic figures can also work as tools of sympathetic magic. Sympathetic magic is the act of connecting a magical object you are working on to influence a target from a distance. A pop culture example of sympathetic magic is a "voodoo doll." In the movies, when a person pricks a voodoo doll with a pin, the target of their magic gets a pain in that part of the body. Sympathetic magic is not all about causing someone pain; it is most often used to influence something in a positive way.

Figural Candle Symbolism

Different figural candles can be used for different kinds of magic. Here are some examples of figural candles and what they can be used for:

Aladdin's Lamp

An Aladdin's Lamp candle is used for intense heartfelt wishes you want to manifest, spiritual or mental enlightenment, or for connecting to or commanding djinn or genies.

Angel

Angel candles are used for protection, blessing, or working with angels and spirit guides.

Ankh

The Ankh is the symbol of life and is used in spells for immortality and is a special symbol of Kemetism and of African cultural identity.

Apple

Apple-shaped candles are used for love spells of any kind—self-love, ensuring a long-lasting committed love, or tempting someone into an illicit and passionate affair. Apple candles are also burned in tribute to Aphrodite, the love goddess, and for fertility, beauty and glamour spells. They can also be used for spells for immortality, youth, and health.

Baphomet

Baphomet, also called the Sabbatic Goat, is used in ceremonial magic and Gnostic ritual as well as in spells to incite wild lust. Baphomet candles can also be used in spells for unifying opposites, in spells of rebellion or freedom, for breaking bad habits, to increase power, or to repel negativity.

Butterfly

Butterfly candles are used for spells of transformation, rebirth, beauty, freedom, evolution. They can be used for connecting to loved ones who have passed on or for cord-cutting or breaking bad habits.

Cat

Cat candles are used in spells where you want to "catch" something or want something to be brought to you. They can also be used for spells to connect to pets, cat spirits, spirit animals, and cat deities. Often, they are used in spells to turn bad luck to good, and in reversing spells.

Cauldron

As the cauldron is first and foremost the symbol of the witch, cauldron candles are used for initiations and rites of passage. Many use these candles for gaining spiritual wisdom. The cauldron is the place of transformation, so it is used in spells for transmutation. It also represents the womb and is used in spells for fertility and pregnancy.

Coffin

Coffin candles are used to end relationships, eliminate difficult situations once and for all, break bad habits, drive unwanted people away, or harm enemies.

Cross

Cross candles are used by Christian practitioners for divine blessings, divine protection, petitioning Jesus, or connecting to Christ consciousness. They can be used as altar candles for spiritualist services, or for uncrossing spells. A cross candle can be used alongside other candles to ensure that your desires are fulfilled as "God's will."

Devil

Devil candles are either used to invoke, drive out, or control the devil or evil spirits. They are also used for commanding and controlling spells as well as curse work. In addition, devil candles can also be used in spells to incite lust, passion, hedonism, debauchery, get fast cash, or have debts repaid.

Divorce/Back-to-Back Couple

This is a candle with a male and female figure facing back to back and is used for separation or break up spells between a couple. It doesn't necessarily have to be for an angry divorce. Depending on the herbs and oils used, it can also be used to peacefully part from someone permanently.

Dog

Dog candles are used in spells to create loyalty, constancy, and faithfulness. They are excellent for spells to attract friendships that will survive the test of time or to ensure the fidelity of a lover. They can also be used for spells to connect to pets and to dog spirits, spirit animals, and dog deities.

Egyptian King/Pharaoh/King Tutankhamen

An Egyptian king candle is used for masculine empowerment, confidence, courage, success, and power over others. It is also used to connect to the spirit of Tutankhamen, other pharaohs, or Egyptian deities.

Egyptian Queen/Queen Nefertiti

An Egyptian queen candle is used for feminine empowerment, confidence, courage, success, and power over others. It is also used to connect to the spirit of Queen Nefertiti, other Egyptian queens, or Egyptian deities.

Embracing Lovers/Lovers' Passion

An embracing lovers candle (sometimes called a lovers' passion candle or a loving couple candle) shows two nude lovers locked in a passionate embrace. It is used in love spells of a sexual nature, sex magic, and spells to invite more passion into a relationship.

Four-Leaf Clover

Four-leaf clover candles are used for general good luck spells, to change bad luck to good, and spells where you would like luck in four areas of your life.

Gargoyle

Gargoyles are old European figures of dragons and other fantasy creatures, and gargoyle candles are used for driving out evil spirits, fierce protection, wealth building, and in spells to call in spiritual guardians.

Goddess of Willendorf/Venus of Willendorf

The Goddess of Willendorf (also called the Venus of Willendorf) is a fertility statue created in 22,000 BCE. Use in spells for abundance, fertility, and connecting with nature, ancestors, past lives, and ancient deities.

Heart

A heart candle is used in spells for passion, romance, healing emotions, empathy, and love between lovers, family, or friends.

Horse

The horse is an ancient symbol of courage, wealth, and success. Use the horse candle in spells for successful ventures, courage, spirit, and connecting to horses, spirit animals, and horse deities.

Horseshoe

The horseshoe is a symbol of ongoing luck. Use a horseshoe candle in spells to support good luck, change bad luck to good, for gambling luck, and to invite continuous luck in a venture or situation.

House

House candles are used for spells to bring peace, love, protection or prosperity into the home, to buy or sell a home, to keep from being evicted, or to find a new living situation.

Laughing Buddha

The Laughing Buddha, also known as Hotei (Japanese) or Budai (Chinese) is a spirit of prosperity and happiness. Use a Laughing Buddha candle for bringing happiness along with abundance, love, health, or any positive purpose.

Lips

Lip-shaped candles are used for spells for opening communication, romance, passion, stopping gossip, and improving speaking skills.

Marriage (Bride-Groom/Bride-Bride/Groom-Groom)

Marriage candles or couples candles are used to get a proposal, have a proposal accepted, strengthen commitment, bless a couple, or improve a marriage. They can also be used in binding spells where one person is bound to another. In other kinds of spells (such as banishing or cleansing spells), they can be used simply to represent a couple.

Mummy

The figure of an Egyptian mummy is used in spells to connect to spirits, past lives, to call on the assistance of ancestors, or to connect to ancient Egypt or Kemetic magic.

Native American Chief/Black Hawk

Native American figural candles are used in spiritualist spells to connect to the spirit of Black Hawk, a war leader of the Sauk tribe. Use a Black Hawk candle for spells of justice, particularly when faced with institutional oppression and if you are connected to Native American ancestry.

Nude Figure

A nude figure of a man or woman represents the authentic self. Use a nude figural candle in a spell to represent yourself or someone you are working on, whether known or unknown. The nude figural candle can also be used in sympathetic magic spells as a spell poppet or what is commonly called a "voodoo" doll.

Owl

An owl candle is used for spells of wisdom, silence, secrets, transition from one state to another, learning, arcane knowledge, or education.

Pan

Pan is the ancient Greek god of nature. Pan candles can be used to celebrate wildness, vitality, sex, lust, fertility, and hedonism. They can also be used in the veneration of Pan.

Phallus/Penis

A phallus candle is used in spells for attraction, sex magic, passion, virility, and control over your own penis or someone else's.

Praying Hands

A praying hands candle is used to amplify and empower prayers and petitions for blessings. It can also be used to enhance meditation, to connect to the divine self within or to connect to deities.

Pyramid

The pyramids of Egypt are impressive, mysterious, and powerful monuments that have stood the test of time. A pyramid candle is used in spells to build wealth, success, power, and strong, long-lasting results in any area of life.

Rose

A rose candle is used to invoke a deep spiritual love or in beauty spells. Roses are used to venerate or invoke Mary, Aphrodite, Adonis, or Santa Muerte. They are also prominent in spiritualist services. Alternatively, they can also be used in spells for confidentiality or to keep secrets from being discovered.

Santa Muerte

Santa Muerte is the Mexican folk saint of the Holy Death. Santa Muerte candles are used for love, fortune, healing, protection and for safe passage to the afterlife. The candles are also used in spells to venerate Santa Muerte.

Seal of Solomon/Star of David
The Seal of Solomon, or Star of David, is a symbol of Judaism. It can be used in spells for alchemy, uniting the elements, protection, blessing, and casting out demons or demonic energy.

Seven-Knob
A seven-knob candle is used in spells of any kind that are cast over seven days. It is used by setting the intention of your spell and then burning one knob each day for seven consecutive days.

Skull
A skull candle is used for spells to affect and influence your own or another person's mind, and for spells to connect to ancestors. It can also be used to open mental or verbal communication, for mental health, to improve intelligence, for wisdom, or for scholarly success.

Sun
A sun candle is used to bring fame, recognition, healing, happiness, for empowerment, and to expose secrets or lies.

Star
A star candle is used to connect to astral realms, for wishes, hopes and dreams, finding your way, and safe travel spells.

The Three Wise Monkeys
The Three Wise Monkeys (Hear No Evil, See No Evil, Speak No Evil) are used in spells to stop gossip, release bad habits, and cultivate right-eous thoughts, speech, and action in yourself or others.

Treasure Chest

Treasure chest candles are used for spells to find hidden treasure, wealth, blessings, and to open up the gifts within.

Virgin of Guadalupe

The Virgin of Guadalupe candle is used for fertility, motherhood, children, blessing spells, and to venerate the Virgin of Guadalupe or to ask for blessings from the Virgin Mary.

Vulva/Vagina

A vulva candle is used in spells for attraction, sex magic, passion, fertility, and control over your own vagina or someone else's.

Witch

A witch candle is used in spells to increase your powers as a magician or to call on a spiritual teacher to bring you more esoteric knowledge. It can also be used in spells of luck, love, reversing, or to receive magical blessings.

Basic Figural Candle Spell

Each figural candle has its specific forte, but it is possible to give a general guideline here for working with a figural candle. In chapter 8, you'll find more complex figural candle workings such as adding support candles and designing layouts.

YOU WILL NEED

Figural candle

Spiritual oil

Dried or powdered herbs

Inscribing tool

Tray or dish

Petition Paper

Glitter (optional)

1. Choose a candle in the shape and color that supports your intention.

2. Inscribe your intentions on the candle. You can write the name of your target or words or phrases (for example, "love," "luck," "perfect health"). Write horizontally across the candle, or write vertically, upward, from base to wick, for things you want to bring in; or downward, from wick toward base, for things you want to clear out.

3. Dress the candle in a spiritual oil that supports your intention by applying several drops of oil to your hand and rubbing it on the surface of the candle. Focus your intention by visualizing your good outcome or speaking your spell words. Feel the energy of your intention moving through your hands and into the candle as you apply it upward for things you want to bring in, or downward for things you want to clear out.

4. Sprinkle an herb or glitter or both on the candle. Dry, light, crumbled, or powdered herbs will adhere the best. Just a light sprinkling is safe and effective in your spell. Glitter is non-flammable and can be added safely.

5. Place your petition paper under your tray.

6. Place your candle on the tray.

7. Sprinkle heavier chunkier herbs around the candle base.

THE SPECIAL MAGIC OF FIGURAL CANDLES

8. Light your candle as you speak your spell words.

9. Snuff your candle out when you go to sleep or leave the house and relight it when you return.

Floating Candle Spells

Floating candles are unique in that they are the only candles designed to be used in spells featuring the element of water. Water is the element of dreams, emotions, and spirits, so if you really want to incorporate the mystical into your spell work, a floating candle spell will allow you to amplify that energy. You can use special waters in the bowl, such as holy water, herbal infusions, water from sacred sources (wells, lakes, ocean, rainwater, melted snow, etc.), or water charged by moonlight. By burning a magic candle in the water, you also imbue the water with the essence of your intention and can use it in baths, to water plants, or in a spray bottle to bless a room.

A Floating Candle Spell

YOU WILL NEED

Bowl or cauldron

Spring water (or any special water)

Fresh flowers aligned with your intention

Gemstones aligned with your intention

Floating candle

Spiritual oil

1. Place gemstones in your bowl or cauldron.

2. Pour your water into the bowl.

3. Float fresh flowers in the water.

4. Dress and bless your candle with a spiritual oil and words of your intention.

5. Float your candle in the water.

6. Light your candle, speaking your intention.

7. Let the candle burn to completion. If you leave the house or go to sleep, snuff the candle, don't blow it out and relight when you awaken or return.

8. Do not use water to put out the candle, it can cause a dangerous fireball.

9. Once the candle has burned completely, remove the flowers and leave them on the earth to thank and bless the earth.

10. Remove the gemstones and place them on your altar or put them away.

11. The water may be returned to the earth, saved for a blessing spray, added to a cleansing bath, or used to water a plant.

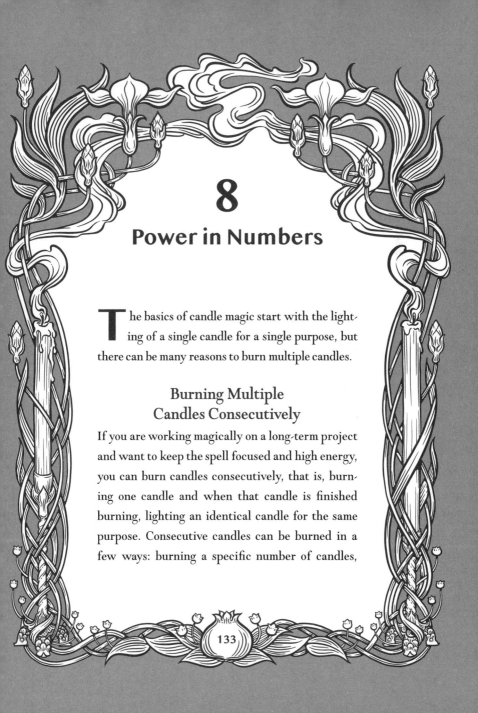

8

Power in Numbers

The basics of candle magic start with the lighting of a single candle for a single purpose, but there can be many reasons to burn multiple candles.

Burning Multiple Candles Consecutively

If you are working magically on a long-term project and want to keep the spell focused and high energy, you can burn candles consecutively, that is, burning one candle and when that candle is finished burning, lighting an identical candle for the same purpose. Consecutive candles can be burned in a few ways: burning a specific number of candles, burning candles for a set time period, or burning candles until the result is achieved.

An example of burning a specific number of candles could be burning seven yellow luck candles, one after the other, for good luck.

An example of burning candles over a set period of time might be for a spell to get a good grade in a class, with the first candle being lit at the beginning of the semester and subsequent candles being burned one after the other until the last day of the semester.

An example for burning a candle until a result is achieved would be a spell to bring in a new lover, with candles being burned one after another until the new love comes into your life.

Burning Multiple Candles Simultaneously

If you are working on more than one spell or working on an issue that has multiple facets, you might want to burn multiple candles at the same time to address the different parts.

Multiple candles can be directed at one spell. For example, you may be doing a spell for financial success and burn one candle for prosperity, another for general success, and a third candle to remove any blocks that may stand in the way.

Multiple candles can also be lit for different spells simultaneously, as long as those spells don't conflict with one another. For example, you could light one candle for a love spell and another candle for a money spell at the same time. You would really be doing two different spells, so it's technically not a multi-candle spell, but I do get asked whether or not it's okay to burn two or more separate candle spells at the same time; I have never found it to cause a problem. Be careful, however. You should avoid doing candle spells with objectives that are at odds with one another. For example, burning two different candles to get two different jobs when you only really want one job divides your attention and projects confusion and lack of focus. In that case, pick the job that you want the most and do a spell for that one, or do a more general spell to get the "best" job.

Burning a Master Candle with Support Candles

You can also burn one main candle, which is called a master candle, with support candles to amplify your intention. Master candles are usually larger, either a larger pillar or a figural candle; support candles are usually smaller and may be arranged around or next to the master candle. Support candles allow us to bring numerology, additional colors, shaped layouts, and more variety and customization into our spell.

You may want to burn a master candle for a certain intention but also bring the power of a certain number into your spell work. For example, to build strong and long-lasting prosperity, you could do a spell with a prosperity master candle surrounded by three smaller support candles for a total of four candles. For more on numerology, see the section below.

Support candles also allow you to add different colors to your spell work, such as a spell with pink and red candles for a heart-centered (pink), yet passionate love (red), or a prosperity spell with green and yellow candles for growth (green) and success (yellow). For more on color magic, see chapter 2.

A setup with a master candle and support candles can also be used to represent different forces and people in a spell. For example, you could have a master candle representing the petition or wish and support candles representing the people for which the wish is intended. Or you could have a master candle representing a deity and one support candle representing the petition and others representing the people who are to receive the benefits of the spell work.

Support candles also allow us to arrange candles in layouts, shaped arrangements that bring an extra layer of meaning to a spell. For example, you could have a master candle for protection surrounded by smaller support candles in a circle to provide a guarding barrier. (For more on layouts, check out chapter 9).

As you get more experienced at candle magic, incorporating more candles into your spells opens up more opportunities for personalizing your spells.

Support Candle to Represent a Person

When choosing a candle to represent another person, there are a couple of options. Most spell casters will choose a figural candle in the shape of a person to represent the individuals involved, but you can also use a taper candle or vigil candle to represent a person. Choose a candle in the color which represents the qualities of that person or the qualities that you wish them to have. Or, if you know the person's birthdate, you can choose a candle in one of the colors that corresponds to their sun sign.

ARIES: red or orange

TAURUS: green or pink

GEMINI: yellow or pale blue

CANCER: silver or white

LEO: gold or purple

VIRGO: brown or green

LIBRA: pink or pale blue

SCORPIO: red or black

SAGITTARIUS: blue or orange

CAPRICORN: black or brown

AQUARIUS: blue or white

PISCES: lavender or pale green

Inscribe the name or initials of the person on the candle to link the energy of the candle to the individual.

Numerology in Candle Spells

Numerology is the study of the symbolism, meaning, and magic of numbers. If you are oriented toward numbers, you may want to include magical numbers in your spell work, as they are another way to give your spells an extra boost of power.

Just as symbols can have magical significance (for example a heart signifying love) numbers have symbolic meaning. We can interpret this magical significance when the numbers are presented to us (for example, when we happen to see a digital clock read 4:44). We can also invoke those numbers when we want to bring in their vibrations. For the most part, we focus on the single digit numbers as power numbers.

1– Beginnings, unity, newness, focused concentration, independence, originality, ambition, will, self-reliance, freedom, strength, initiative, new ventures, essence, identity, peace.

2– Duality, partnership, division, choice, cooperation, harmony, support, diplomacy, patience, parenting, nurturing, home, marriage, romantic love, contrast.

3– Trinity, union of the divine and human, expression, creativity, optimism, enthusiasm, joy, family, fertility, children, talent, communication, writing, movement, time.

4– Material concerns, practicality, orderliness, logic, hard work, loyalty, building, responsibility, foundations, concentration, patience, endurance, health, job, real estate.

5– Adventure, adaptability, change, freedom, exploration, variety, sensuality, curiosity, travel, imagination, versatility, legal issues.

6– Beauty, harmony, balance, nurturing, understanding, healing, duty, comfort, service, community, romance, justice, chance.

7– Spirituality, good luck, philosophy, wisdom, faith, divine nature, invention, contemplation, introspection, esotericism, perfection, authority, public image, religion.

8– Achievement, strength, self-discipline, power, success, authority, manifestation, ambition, attainment, renewal, money, prosperity, career.

9– Completion, culmination, wishes coming true, change, graduation, evolution, next steps, endings.

There are two special numbers that will show up in magic that are outside of the 1 through 9 range.

11– Master number, prophecy, intuition, enlightenment, adaptability, sensitivity, awareness, psychic ability.

13— Luck, success despite long odds, transformation, magic, manifestation.

There are several ways to incorporate these numbers into your spell work and add another level of intention to your magic.

Multi-Candle Spells

You can do a multi-candle spell and use the number of candles that supports your spell work. For example, a fertility spell using three different candles simultaneously or a prosperity spell with four single candles burned consecutively.

Burning a Single Candle Over a Certain Number of Days

You can also burn candles over several days and choose a number of days that has numerological significance. For example, you could burn a seven-knob candle over seven days or you could work with a tall taper candle and burn it over nine days.

Burning a Candle for a Certain Period of Time

Instead of burning a candle for a measured segment over a certain number of days, you can time your candle to burn for a certain number of minutes or hours each day. If you choose this method, you will not be able to control the number of days the candle is burned.

Starting a Candle at a Certain Time

Another way to incorporate numerology into your spell work is to start your candle spell at a certain hour, either starting on the hour (for example at 8:00) or choosing a repeating number such as 2:22.

Adding a Certain Number of Herbs to Your Spell

As you add herbs to your spell, you may want to consider the number of herbs or curios you use in your spell. For example, you may want to add seven herbs to a spell to connect to your spirit guides.

Working with Numbers on a Vigil Candle

If you're dressing a vigil candle and poking holes around the wick, the default number is seven, however, if you want to use a different number that more closely aligns with your intention, you can do that to amplify the energy of your spell.

Other Ways of Working Numerology into Your Spell

When working with numbers, we have only discussed choosing a number that corresponds to your intention. However, you can work with other special numbers such as dates, addresses, lucky numbers, and so on.

How to Work with Multiple Digits

Whenever you get to a number that has two or more digits, we can use them in two ways: looking at each digit individually or adding the digits together to reduce them to a single master number. So, for example, if you have a number 21, you can use the energy of the 2 and the 1, and then you can add $2 + 1$, which equals 3.

When getting into dates, such as birthdates, anniversaries, or potential dates to start your spell work, the method is to add the numbers of the day, month, and year together and reduce them to their single number. For example, the date July, 4, 1776 is $7+4+1+7+7+6 = 32$. 32 needs to be further reduced: $3+2 = 5$. So the number to work with to access the energy of this date is 5.

Working with Numerology and Dates to Start Your Spell

Numerology lends itself very well to working with dates. You can work with numerology to choose the date to start your candle spell. If you  want to do a spell to support the successful manifestation of a project and decided to work with the number eight, for example, you can wait until you get to an "eight" day to start your spell. The simplest way to do this is to wait until a day of the month that reduces to eight, such as the 8th, 17th (1+7 = 8), or 26th (2+6 = 8) of the month. If you'd like to get into more complex numerology, you can add the month and year into the mix and reduce to eight. If you are looking for a spell start date that completely reduces to an 8, the way to do this is to first start with the current date.

Today is the 4th of June, 2020

$4 + 6 + 2 + 0 + 2 + 0 = 14$

$14 = 1+4 = 5$

So, today would be a 5 day.

Once you determine the number of today's date, you can just add 1 for each additional day

5 June, 2020 = 6

6 June, 2020 = 7

7 June, 2020 = 8

So, working with numerology, the nearest upcoming eight day after our start date would be June 7, 2020.

Blending Numerology with Other Factors

If you want to add even more power to your spell launch date, you can incorporate moon phases, moon signs, astrology, time of starting and so on, in addition to numerology. For example, you could start a love spell on a two day that lands on a Friday, with a waxing moon in the sign of Taurus at 2:22 a.m.

Whew, that's a lot! Most spell casters don't get that complex with their spell's start time. Don't feel as though you must work to that level of detail. Working with one or two timing methods is just fine.

Working with Special Dates

Another way of working with numerology and dates can be to come up with special numbers regarding dates.

If you are doing a spell to influence a person, you can use the birth-date of that person, reduce it to a single number and do a spell incorporating that number of candles or herbs to add another layer of connection to the person. You can also work with anniversaries in the same way.

This kind of numerology can also be used on things not related to people. If you were applying to get a job at a corporation, for example, you might use the founding date of that corporation in your spell work to influence them to hire you.

Working with Addresses

Another interesting way to work the power of numbers into your spell is through the power of the address number on a house or building. If your spell involves buying or selling a home, renting an apartment, getting a job at a certain location, or something else associated with a building, you can create a deep connection with the location by incorporating the key number for the address into your spell work.

Just reduce the numbers in the address to a single number and incorporate that number into your spell work through the number of candles, number of days the candle burns, or number of herbs used on the candle. For example, if the address is 2509 Main Street Unit 7, add $2+5+0+9+7 = 23$, then reduce $2+3 = 5$. Use this key number 5 in the spell work to connect to the location in a powerful way.

Lucky Numbers

Many people have a favorite number they consider to be their lucky number. You can use your lucky number in spells for yourself to enhance and empower the connection between yourself and your spell work, or someone else's lucky number if you are doing a spell for them to empower the connection between the work and the person.

Multi-Day Spells

Multi-day candle spells can be done by burning one candle in segments over the course of a set number of days or can be done by burning individual candles, one each day, over the course of a certain number of days.

Multi-day spell done with a single candle

A single candle spell burned over multiple days can be done with any candle with the one precaution that you must choose a candle of the appropriate size for the number of days you hope to burn it. It's hard to make a birthday candle burn more than one day, and it's impossible to burn a vigil candle or a large pillar candle in less than a few days.

There are some different methods of burning a candle over a certain number of days. The easiest method is to just estimate and burn the candle for an approximate amount over each of the days. If you'd like to be more precise, before you start your spell, you could scratch marks creating segments in the wax and burn it down to the mark each day. Another way to mark off these segments is with straight pins. Still another alternative is to get a candle especially created to burn in segments.

Some candles are especially designed to be burned over several days. A seven-knob candle is a single candle made up of seven individual segments. The idea behind the seven-knob candle is that you burn one segment each day over the course of seven days.

Multi-Day Spell Done with a Seven-Knob Candle

YOU WILL NEED

Seven-knob candle

Dish or tray

Wax inscribing tool

Spiritual oil

Dried herbs

Glitter

Snuffer

1. Inscribe your intentions on the candle. You can write one single word or a short phrase seven times—once on each of the knobs (for example, "love," "luck," "health")—or you can write seven different words or phrases, a different one on each knob, as long as they all pertain to one spell. Write across the candle horizontally, or write vertically: up from base to wick for things you want to bring in, or down from wick to base for things you want to clear out.

2. Dress the candle in a spiritual oil that supports your intention by applying several drops of oil to your hand and rubbing it on the surface of the candle. Again, apply it up from base to wick for things you want to bring in, or down from wick to base, for things you want to clear out.

3. As you apply the oil and hold the candle, visualize your magical goal, speak your spell words, and feel the energy moving from your hands into the candle.

4. Sprinkle an herb, glitter (or both) on the candle. Dry, light powdered herbs will adhere the best. Chunkier, heavier herbs such as roots or resin pieces might need to be ground up in a mortar and pestle before sticking to the candle. Don't overdo it with the herbs. Some herbs are flammable and will catch fire as your candle burns. Just a light sprinkling is safe and effective in your spell. Most glitter is nonflammable and can be added safely.

5. Place your candle on the tray. If you are having trouble getting the candle to remain steady, you can warm the bottom of the candle with a match or lighter and then press it onto the tray.

6. Sprinkle any heavier herbs around the candle's base.

Seven-Knob Candle and Taper Candle with Pins Marking Segments

7. Light your candle as you speak your petition.

8. When one knob has completely burned, snuff out your candle.

9. On the following day, light your candle again and burn another knob and then snuff the candle when it's complete.

10. Repeat steps 7 through 9, burning one knob each day until the final knob is lit. Let the candle burn to completion.

 ## Taper Candle Spell
Divided into Segments with Pins

Multi-day candle spells can also be done with plain taper candles and straight pins. Using straight pins, divide the taper candle into equal segments by pushing pins into the side. In the next example is a working that spans three days, but you can adapt it to the number of days that best corresponds with your intention.

YOU WILL NEED

Tall beeswax taper candle

Dish or flat tray

Spiritual oil

Dried herbs

Glitter

Three straight pins

Snuffer

1. Dress the candle in a spiritual oil that supports your intention by applying several drops of oil to your hand and rubbing it on the surface of the candle. Apply it up from base to wick for things you

want to bring in, or down from wick to base for things you want to clear out.

2. Sprinkle an herb, glitter (or both) on the candle. Dry, light powdered herbs will adhere the best. Chunkier, heavier herbs such as roots or resin pieces might need to be ground up in a mortar and pestle before sticking to the candle. Just a light sprinkling is safe and effective in your spell. Most glitter is nonflammable and can be added safely.

3. Estimate or measure about one third of the way down from the top of the candle and push a pin into the side of the candle.

4. Measure another third of the way down and insert a pin into the side of the candle.

5. Finally, push the last pin into the base of the candle, almost at the bottom.

6. Warm the base of the candle with a match or lighter to slightly melt the wax and affix it to the tray or dish.

7. Speak your spell words and light the candle.

8. On day one, allow one segment to burn until the pin drops and then snuff the candle out.

9. On the second day, burn another segment until the second pin drops and then snuff out the candle.

10. On the third day, let the candle burn completely.

11. Once the candle spell is complete, you can retrieve the pins and use them to keep the energy of the spell going. The typical way to work with pins is to hide them by pinning them in curtains,

under furniture, in carpeting, or in the lining of clothing to keep the magical influence flowing.

Burning Candles without Measurements

Of course, you always have the option to burn a portion of any candle each day over a specific number of days just by estimation; you don't have to use knobs or pins or be precise in measuring the segments burned each day. For example, if you decide you want to burn a candle for three days, you can let it burn for *about* a third each day, finally allowing it to burn completely on the third day. Of course for a bit more precision, you can mark off segments before you prepare the candle using an inscriber to make lines in the side of the candle, or mark the sides of the glass with a paint pen for glass-encased candles and use these as a rough guide.

It bears repeating that if you are thinking of burning a candle in segments, the one thing you may want to take into consideration is that if you have a large candle such as a vigil candle or a large pillar, it will be better to burn it over a greater number of days. You won't be able to burn a large candle completely in two or three days.

Multi-Day and Multi-Candle Spell

Multi-day spells can be done with individual candles over several days. You can choose to burn several versions of the same candle for a series of days or you can burn different candles toward a single goal.

The goal is to complete a candle each day, so make sure any candles you choose are small enough to burn within 24 hours. The ideal candles for this kind of work are slim tapers, which are the same size as chime candles or Hanukkah candles; tiny tapers, which are birthday candle size; or tea lights. Small votive candles and thick tapers, which are the same thickness as regular tapers but about 5" (12 cm) tall, can be used, but since they may burn for several hours may be more difficult to manage in terms of making sure that you are able to burn one completely each day.

 ## Multi-Day Multi-Candle Spell with the Same Candle Type

YOU WILL NEED

Several small candles of the same color and style

Cookie sheet, dish or flat tray

Spiritual oil

Dried herbs

Glitter (optional)

1. Dress each of the candles in a spiritual oil that supports your intention by applying several drops of oil to your hand and rubbing it on the surface of the candle. Apply it up from base to wick for things you want to bring in, or down from wick to base for things that you want to clear out.

2. Sprinkle an herb or glitter (or both) on each candle. Dry, light powdered herbs will adhere the best. Chunkier, heavier herbs such as roots or resin pieces might need to be ground up in a mortar and pestle before sticking to the candle. Just a light sprinkling

is safe and effective in your spell. Most glitter is nonflammable and can be added safely.

3. Warm the bottom of each candle with a match or lighter and then press it onto the tray. You may place the candles in a layout that supports your intention.

4. Light the first candle as you speak your petition.

5. Let the candle burn until it's complete. If you have to leave or go to sleep before your candle is complete, snuff your candle out (don't blow it out) and then relight it when you return.

6. On the following day, light your second candle and let it burn until it is complete.

7. Keep repeating until you have burned all your candles.

Multi-Day, Multi-Candle Spells with Several Different Candles

It is also possible to burn several candles of different colors over the course of several days. As long as they all support the same goal, they are part of the same spell. This is usually done for spells where there is a natural progression of some kind.

An example of this could be to do a spell for a job and lighting candles for confidence, prosperity, open roads, and success.

Another example is a spell to mend a relationship where candles are burned to clear out negativity, heal old hurts, open up communication, bring in reconciliation, and rekindle romance.

When preparing this kind of spell, think of each candle as being a step on a road. As you create your plan, think about the first step, the next, and the next, and finally the culmination of your spell.

Multi-Day Spell Done with Different Candles

YOU WILL NEED

Several small candles in colors that support different aspects of your intention

Cookie sheet, dish, or flat tray

Several spiritual oils

Dried herbs

Glitter

1. Plan your spell in advance and determine the order of the candles and the goal of each candle.

2. Dress each of the candles in the spiritual oil that supports its intention. Apply several drops of oil to your hand and rub it on the surface of the candle. Apply it up from base to wick for things you want to bring in, or down from wick to base for things that you want to clear out.

3. Choose the intention of each individual candle and sprinkle the herbs or glitter (or both) on each candle. Dry, light powdered herbs will adhere the best. Just a light sprinkling is safe and effective in your spell. Most glitter is nonflammable and can be added safely.

4. Warm the bottom of each candle with a match or lighter and then press it onto the tray. You may place the candles in a layout that supports your intention.

5. Light the first candle as you speak your petition.

6. Let the candle burn until it is spent. If you have to leave or go to sleep before your candle is complete, snuff your candle out (don't blow it out) and relight it when you return.

7. On the following day, light your second candle and let it burn until it is complete.

8. Keep repeating until you have burned all your candles.

With all multi-candle multi-day spells, you are not required to set your candles up all at once. You could easily prepare, set up, and burn one each day in a candle holder, for example.

9

Candle Spell Layouts

Candle spells have the option of layouts; that is, positioning the candles in a way to create a shape or design that also supports your candle work. Layouts can be created with multiple candles or by creating shapes with sprinkled sachet powders or herbs. Layouts can be created simply to be visually appealing or they can be designed to add a specific intention to your spell work.

To map out a layout, you need to look at your spell from a bird's-eye view, looking down at your tray or altar space from above. An easy-to-imagine example of creating a layout would be with a spell using three candles. Three candles could be arranged on a tray in a line of three in a row or in a triangle shape.

To make a layout, observe your candles from above and arrange them in a shape. Some people like to set a central candle (such as a large pillar or a figural candle) on a tray and position smaller support candles around in a shape. You can also sprinkle herbs and sachet powders on your dish or tray next to or between candles to reinforce these shapes, or just use a single candle with herbs or powders sprinkled on the tray to create some of the more complex shapes.

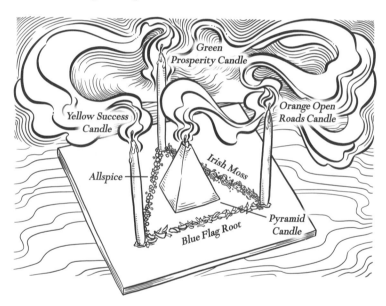

Candle Spell Layout Example

Shapes and Symbols

Each design you might select for your layout can have a particular meaning that can amplify the power of your spell.

Arrow

Direction, movement, unification, separation.

Arrows can be laid out pointing up, down, left, or right; each with its own meaning.

Point Up

Forceful movement, direction, expressive power, building strong foundations, ascension, hierarchy.

Point Down

Receptivity, drawing something in, bringing spiritual knowledge down to earth.

Point Right

Moving forward in time, progress, new ventures, travel.

Point Left

Looking backward, revisiting, going back to a better time, sending things backward, revision, history, healing the past.

Two-Headed Arrows (One Point on Each End)

Two arrows or a two-headed arrow pointed away from each other signify two or more elements moving away from each other, separation, or break-ups. Two arrows or a two-headed arrow pointed toward each other signify two or more elements moving toward each other, reunion, or unification.

Circle

Unity, completion, wholeness, harmony, never-ending, infinity, cycles, perfection, enlightenment, protection, cycle of rebirth, spirit, fertility, luck, commitment.

Circles can be laid out with the candles or drawn around candles with herbs or sachets to give definition; joining with other elements (anything inside the circle) and separating other elements (anything outside the circle).

Cross

The four elements (air, fire, water, earth), four directions (east, south, west, north), the meeting of spiritual and material, intersections, crossroads, Christianity, Christ consciousness, banishing.

Cross layouts can be used to symbolically place something at the crossroads—that is, call in spirits to give blessings and assist with your spell. They can also be used to either cast something out into the wider world or to send your spell intention out to be seen in the wider world. Sometimes crosses are used to "X" out something unwanted. Pagans, Wiccans, and those who spiritually connect to the four elements or four directions can also use a cross layout to section out special candles in each quadrant.

Crown

Power, royalty, divine blessing, success, mastery, attainment, achievement, wisdom.

Laying your candles or herbs and powders in a crown pattern (a flat line for the base of the crown with a zig zag line above for the points of the crown) is used to bring in power and success. Generally, the layout includes three points on the crown, but if you have a spell with several intentions (for example, "I am successful, wealthy, healthy, respected, and famous"), you can create a crown with a point for each intention and set a candle at each point for those particular intentions.

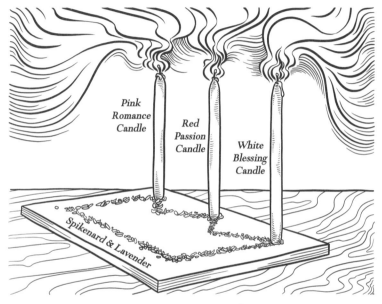

Crown Layout Example

Diamond

Wealth, action in two directions, "as above, so below," manifestation, transformation.

A diamond shape combines the stability of a square (four sides) with the dynamic nature of the triangle. You may create your diamond by fusing two triangles together (a diamond with a line through the middle) or just outlining the four sides.

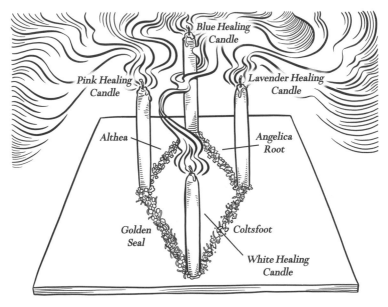

Diamond Layout Example

Eye

The All-Seeing Eye, protection from the evil eye, second sight, psychic awareness, opening of the third eye.

An eye-shaped layout is used for spells where you are either protecting from the evil eye, opening up spiritual vision, or wanting to keep an eye on something or someone.

Heart

Love, romance, emotional healing, marriage, soothing a broken heart, reconciliation, lust, family love, friendship, love of humanity, heart chakra opening.

Heart shapes are most often used in romantic love spells, and can be used to attract a new love or to build on an existing one. However, hearts can also be used for other kinds of love, including opening the heart to giving and receiving good friendships and harmonious family relations.

Hexagon

Work, job, industriousness, community, group efforts, harmony, order, business, new ventures, protection, truth, manifestation.

The hexagon is sacred geometry; and its shape is found in nature, most recognizably in the shape of honeycomb cells and snowflakes. Using this pattern in spells for businesses, groups, and organizations helps them to flow harmoniously and effortlessly toward a common goal.

Lemniscate (Infinity Symbol)

Infinite energy, connection to divine enlightenment, magic, manifestation, past lives and future lives, never-ending growth.

The lemniscate is a figure eight on its side and represents the idea of infinity. Much like a circle, it represents never-ending cycles but has a more dynamic quality of building and acceleration. The point where the figure eight crosses over itself also incorporates the qualities of the cross. Use this symbol when you want your outcome to be ongoing and growing.

Line

Division, separation, connection, movement, a path, open roads, travel, growth, direction.

Lines can be created in layouts either horizontally (for stability) or vertically (for dynamic energy). Straight lines represent directness. Wavy lines represent overcoming obstacles, finding one's way, psychic links, and spiritual connection.

Lines drawn with sachet powders or herbs can be used to connect two or more things or can be used to separate them.

Octagon

Transition, renewal, regeneration, rebirth.

Octagons can be used in spells where you desire change or the renewal of something that has died out.

Pentagon

The five elements, manifestation, creativity, travel, free-spiritedness, freedom, spiritual over material.

Pentagons are used in spells to invoke the five elements (air, fire, water, earth, spirit) or to focus on a material manifestation. They are also excellent for spells to increase creative flow or openness.

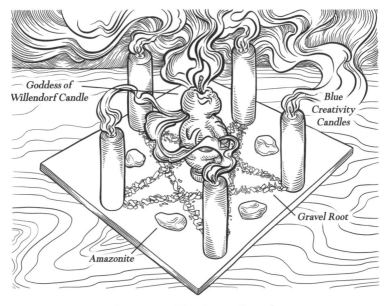

Pentagon and Star Layout Example

Rectangle

Movement toward structure, reliability, stability, order, authority, longevity, communication, messages, four elements (see Square).

Rectangles share many of the same qualities as squares with the added element of movement. Place your candles in a horizontal rectangle to create more harmony or in a vertical rectangle to bring more dynamic energy to your spell work.

Spiral

Invoking/banishing, inward/outward spiritual journey, shamanism, altered states of consciousness, meditation.

Spirals are an ancient symbol and represent the connection to the inner and outer worlds. Create a layout that spirals clockwise for spells to connect to your inner self or for invoking. Working with a counterclockwise spiral is ideal for bringing the inner spiritual life to the conscious level and for banishing.

Square

Structure, reliability, stability, order, authority, longevity, four elements, home, blocking, binding, protection, comfort.

Squares are used for spells where structure and stability are important. When doing a spell where you want something strong and long-lasting or you want authority to be respected, laying out a square will bring that defined energy.

Star

Fame, recognition, happiness, good fortune, luck, divine connection, protection, human body, connection between the material and the spiritual, manifestation, health, wisdom, spiritual guidance.

Stars of all kinds represent connection to divine energy. Stars with a certain number of points can also be used for their numerological value.

The five-pointed star (pentagram) with the point upright represents the human body with head and extended arms and legs or the five elements. Pentagrams represent protection, manifestation in the material world and the element of earth.

The six-pointed star (Seal of Solomon) represents the combination of the four elements, the fusing of duality or the Seal of Solomon and can therefore be used in spells for manifestation, reconciliation, or spiritual wisdom. It's especially meaningful as a symbol of Judaism.

Triangle

Trinity, past-present-future, body-mind-spirit, summoning of spirits, direction, movement, alchemy symbols of the four elements.

Triangles contain the magic number three as well as the idea of movement. The subtleties of this movement can be expressed in the direction that the triangle's point is facing.

Point Up

Forceful movement, expressive power, strong foundations building up, ascension, hierarchy, success, spiritual expansion.

Point Down

Receptivity, drawing something in, bringing spiritual knowledge down to earth, manifestation.

Point Right

Moving forward in time, progress, new ventures, travel.

Point Left

Looking backward, revisiting, going back to a better time, sending things backward, revising history, healing the past.

Using Multiple Shapes in Layouts

With any spell, you can mix and match shapes. Place the candles in a layout of one shape and sprinkle herbs and powders in other shapes to bring dimension, richness, and beauty to your spell work.

Direction

Putting candles in the directions of north, south, east, and west can add another combination of elements to your spell work layout. These directions can be discerned with a compass, or you can use the symbolic directions of north being the top of your plate (away from you, the viewer), south being the bottom of the plate (closest to you), east to the right, and west to the left.

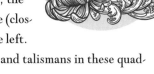

Placing particular candle colors, herbs, and talismans in these quadrants adds detailed energy to your spells.

East

Items placed in the east can be used to influence conscious ideas, thought and communication. It's also great for new beginnings, written or spoken words, mental influence over others and fresh inspiration.

South

Items placed in the south can be charged to create movement, action, energy, passion, and will. Placing items here will create motivation, influence how you or others act and move in the world and is great for getting the action going.

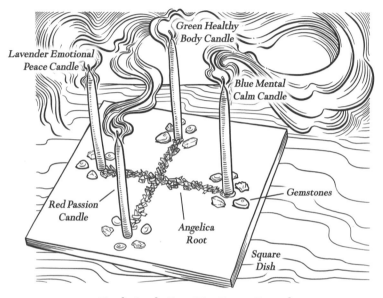

North, South, East, West Layout Example

West

Items placed in the west connect to the spiritual, psychic, mystical and deep emotional realms. Use this direction to influence the subconscious, dreams, and beliefs, or to contact the spirit world or divine energy.

North

Items placed in the north influence the material world: objects, money, the body, places, buildings, ownership, physical health. The north represents physical manifestations, so if you are working to get a "thing" of some kind, this is the perfect direction to focus your energies.

Moving Candle Spells

Moving candle spells are multi-candle, multi-day layout spells where the candles are moved each day. The goal of a moving candle spell is to move one or more candles across the tray either toward or away from another candle.

An example of a moving candle spell could be working to bring in more money, with individual candles representing sources of income moving toward a candle representing you. Another could be doing a spell to clear negative people out of your life by having a candle representing you and a candle to represent each of the people that you want to banish and having them move away from one another.

The classic example of a moving candle spell is a seven-day "Come to Me" spell where two candles are set up, one representing yourself and one representing your target. As each day passes, you move the candles step-by-step, closer together until the last bits are touching one another and burn to completion on the seventh day.

Come to Me Moving Candle Spell

YOU WILL NEED

Two nude figural candles—one representing you and one representing your target

Cookie sheet, long serving dish, or tray

Spiritual oil for love, attraction, or commitment

Dried herbs for attraction such as catnip, damiana, cinnamon, ginger, or patchouli

Glitter

Inscribing tool

1. Choose a male or female candle to represent yourself and another to represent your target. Select colors that support your intention. They can both be of the same color or each be different colors.

2. Inscribe your name horizontally on the front of the base of the candle that represents you and your target's name across the base of the candle that represents them.

3. Dress the candles in a spiritual oil for love by applying several drops of oil to your hand and rubbing it on the surface of the candle. You will want to apply it "up," from base to wick, because this particular spell work is meant to bring in love. Visualize your good outcome and feel the energy in your hands radiating and charging your candles.

4. Sprinkle glitter on the candles.

5. Place the candles facing each other at either end of your tray.

6. Sprinkle a path of herbs in a line between the two candles.

7. Light your target's candle first (to activate them first) and then your candle second as you speak your intention.

8. Let the candles burn about one-seventh of the way down and then snuff them out. Snuff out your candle first and your target's candle second.

9. If, while the candles are burning, you notice one candle burning faster than the other, snuff the faster burning candle out so that the slower burning one can catch up.

10. Always snuff your candles out when you go to sleep or leave the house.

11. On the following day, move each of your candles toward each other along the path of herbs about one-seventh of the way closer together.

12. Light your candles again and burn them about one-seventh of the way down.

13. Repeat for each of the seven days with the candles representing you and your target moving closer together. If your candles drip and stick to the tray, use a butter knife or similar object to lift them off the tray. Don't worry if some of the wax drips get left behind as you move your candles closer.

14. On the seventh day, make sure to move the last bit of the two candles together as closely as possible (they may have to overlap to be touching) and let them burn completely.

Diagram of Come to Me Moving Candle Spell

Moving candle spells are a powerful ritual to bring things or people closer together, moving them apart or moving them in unison. If you are planning a multi-day spell, you can incorporate moving candles to highlight the movement element of your spell.

Some Examples of Moving Candle Spells:

Moving a person toward a career goal

Moving a prize or gift toward a person

Moving a person toward or away from a location

Moving clients toward a business

Moving bad luck away from a person or place

Moving a couple toward a new home

Moving two lovers closer together or moving them apart

Moving prosperity toward a person

Moving a person toward health

Moving a person toward an as yet unknown soulmate or vice versa

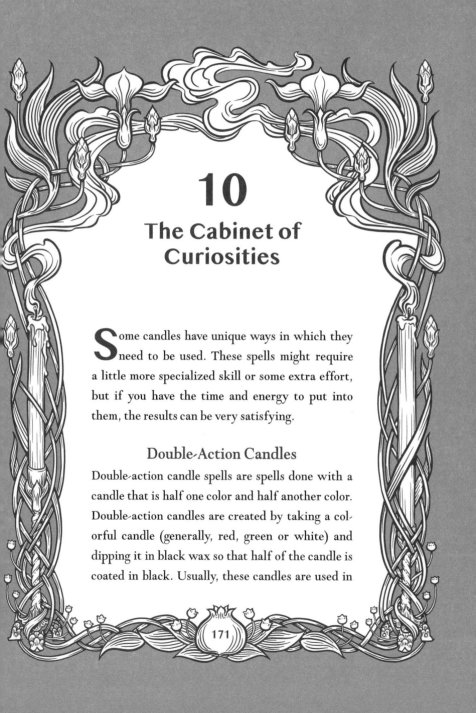

10
The Cabinet of Curiosities

Some candles have unique ways in which they need to be used. These spells might require a little more specialized skill or some extra effort, but if you have the time and energy to put into them, the results can be very satisfying.

Double-Action Candles

Double-action candle spells are spells done with a candle that is half one color and half another color. Double-action candles are created by taking a colorful candle (generally, red, green or white) and dipping it in black wax so that half of the candle is coated in black. Usually, these candles are used in reversing spells that are meant to send negativity back to its source and to enhance good luck. These spells are like burning two separate candles, a black one for reversing or removing the negativity and one of another color for bringing in something positive. The fact that you do the spell with a single candle amplifies the connection between the two spells and symbolically creates a stronger link.

Whenever you are burning a double-action candle for a reversing spell, you need to consider which half of the candle to burn first. Like a regular spell, you would want to work on sending back the negativity before bringing in your blessings, so it would be best to burn the black half of the candle before burning the colorful half. If your candle is set up with the black half at the top already, your candle is ready to dress with oil and light. If the colorful half is at the top, you will have to carve the candle to turn it upside down and create a new top and bottom to the candle. This action in itself is not pointless extra work—the act of turning the candle around can be incorporated into your ritual, in effect turning the situation around and reversing the negative energy and sending it back to its source.

 ## Double-Action Candle Spell *Without* Carving a New Top/Base

YOU WILL NEED

Double-action candle that is black on top and another color at the bottom

Small mirror

Dish or tray

Inscribing tool

Reverse Negativity oil

Love, prosperity or other blessing oil of some kind

Sulfur

Powdered herb for love, prosperity, or other blessing

1. Choose a candle color that is most closely aligned with your objective. For example, a half red/half black candle for sending back negativity about a love situation, a half green/half black for sending back negativity surrounding a job or money or a half white/half black for reversing negativity and bringing in blessings of any kind.

2. Using your inscribing tool, write what it is that you would like to get rid of on the black half. Alternatively, if you know the source of the negativity, you may inscribe the person's name or, if unknown, "my enemies" on the candle. When you inscribe these words, you can amplify the clearing effect by writing them in a downward direction (from wick toward the middle of the candle) to clear out. You can empower them still more by writing them in reverse (mirror writing).

3. On the lower half of the candle, the part that is colorful, you can inscribe the words of what you would like to bring in and/or inscribe your name. Because you are bringing something in, write these in an upward direction (from base toward the middle of the candle). These should be written in the normal direction, *not* mirror writing.

4. Put a few drops of Reverse Negativity oil on your hands and rub your hands together. Apply the oil to the black half of the candle in a downward motion (from wick toward the middle of the candle). Visualize sending any negativity back to its source and charge the candle with your energy.

5. Wash your hands and then apply a few drops of your blessing oil to your hands and rub them together. Apply the oil to the colorful half of the candle in an upward motion (from the base toward the middle of the candle). Visualize receiving your blessings and charge the candle with your energy.

6. Sprinkle sulfur on the black half of the candle.

7. Sprinkle your powdery herb on the colorful half of the candle.

8. Place your candle on top of a small mirror. If you are having difficulties getting your candle to stand upright on the mirror, you can melt the wax on the bottom of the candle with a match and affix it to the mirror. Place the mirror and candle on a dish or tray.

9. Speak your spell words and light the candle.

10. Burn the candle while you are at home and awake. If you leave the house or go to sleep, snuff the candle out and relight it when you are able to keep an eye on it.

❦ Double-Action Candle Spell ❧ Carving a New Top/Base

If you have a candle with the colorful part at the top of the candle, you'll have to "butt the candle" or turn the candle upside down and make the top the base and make a new top out of the former base.

Before you start, assess the candle. If the top of the candle has a point of some kind that will prevent it from sitting flat on a dish or tray, you will have to carve off that point so that it can be the new bottom of the candle.

No matter what, you will have to carve a new top out of the bottom so the wick is exposed and you can light the candle.

YOU WILL NEED

Double-action candle that is black on the bottom and another color
at the top

Paring knife or pen knife

Small mirror

Dish or tray

Inscribing tool

Reverse Negativity oil

Love, prosperity, or other blessing oil of some kind

Sulfur

Powdered herb for love, prosperity, or other blessing

1. Choose a candle color most closely aligned with your objective.

2. With a knife, first cut off the top of the candle to make it flat so
   that it can be the new base of the candle.

3. Next, carve away the bottom of the candle so that it can be the
   new top. Take care to carve around the wick without cutting it.
   Leave at least ¼" (6 mm) of wick exposed to light the candle.

4. Using your inscribing tool, write what it is that you would like
   to get rid of on the black half. Alternatively, if you know the
   source of the negativity, you may inscribe the person's name or, if
   unknown, "my enemies" on the candle. When you inscribe these
   words, you can amplify the clearing effect by writing them in a
   downward direction (from wick toward the middle of the candle). You can empower them still more by writing the letters in
   reverse (mirror writing).

5. On the lower half of the candle, the part that is colorful, you can inscribe the words of what you would like to bring in and/ or inscribe your name. Because you are bringing something in, you may want to write these in an upward direction (from base toward the middle of the candle). These should be written in the normal direction, *not* mirror writing.

6. Put a few drops of the Reverse Negativity oil on your hands and rub your hands together. Apply the oil to the black half of the candle in a downward motion (from wick toward the middle of the candle). Visualize sending all negativity back to its source and charge the candle with your energy.

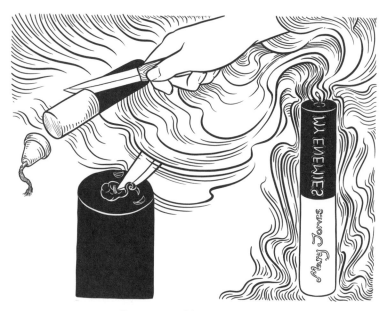

Carving a Double Action Candle

7. Wash your hands and then apply a few drops of your blessing oil to your hands and rub them together. Apply the oil to the colorful half of the candle in an upward motion (from the base toward the middle of the candle). Visualize your blessings coming to you and charge the candle with your energy.

8. Sprinkle sulfur on the black half of the candle.

9. Sprinkle your powdery herb on the colorful half of the candle.

10. Place your candle on top of a small mirror. If you are having difficulties getting your candle to stand upright on the mirror, you can melt the wax on the bottom of the candle with a match and affix it to the mirror.

11. Speak your spell words and light the candle.

12. Burn the candle while you are at home and awake. If you leave the house or go to sleep, snuff the candle out and relight it when you are able to keep an eye on it.

Oil Lamps

While technically not candles, oil lamps share many of the same qualities and are a good alternative for magical work. One of the advantages of oil lamps is that they can be refilled over and over again, which is great for spell work that is ongoing. For example, if you want ongoing and continually growing prosperity, you can create an oil lamp and keep your abundance going rather than lighting one candle or burning candle after candle.

There are several ways to create oil lamps—with a kerosene lamp, a mason jar, or a ghee or olive oil lamp. The mason jar lamp is simple to make and can be put together with easy-to-find, inexpensive items.

 **Mason Jar Oil Lamp**

YOU WILL NEED

Mason jar

Metal mason jar lid with a hole poked into it

Dish or tray

Olive oil

Roll of cotton gauze bandages

Chopstick or fork

Spiritual oil that supports your intention

Herbs, roots, gemstones, and/or talismans that support your intention

Photo and/or petition paper

Personal concerns (hair, fingernail clippings or anything with a
   target's DNA)

Scissors

Tweezers

Screwdriver

1. Open your mason jar and put gemstones, talismans, herbs, photos, personal concerns, petition papers, and a few drops of your spiritual oil in the jar. As you add each element, you can speak words of what you would like it to bring to your spell. The objective here is not to fill the jar with objects, just a few of these things are fine.

2. Fill the jar with olive oil to about 1" (25 mm) from the brim.

3. Cut a 24" (60 cm) long section of cotton gauze and begin to roll it lengthwise into a long "snake." This will be your wicking. You won't be able to roll it completely tight, but roll it as tightly as you can.

4. Coil the wicking into the jar. As you do this, use your chopstick or fork to push the wicking down into the jar as it absorbs the oil. You can also push down any herbs that have floated to the top as well.

5. Top off the jar with more oil until it reaches about ¼" (6 mm) from the top.

Mason Jar Oil Lamp

6. Poke a hole in your lid with a large nail and then work the hole to be larger with a screwdriver. Or, if you have an old fashioned beer can opener (called a can tapper), you can make a triangle

THE CABINET OF CURIOSITIES

sized hole of the right size in your lid. The hole in your lid should be about ¼" (6 mm) in diameter. Alternatively, you can purchase decorative Mason jar lid inserts that already have holes for converting mason jars into straw sippers, lotion bottles, or other cute and decorative things. Just make sure you're using a metal lid and not a plastic one, because plastic and fire don't mix.

7. Poke the wicking through the lid so that about ½" (12 mm) is sticking above the lid. Light the wicking and trim it back to about ¼" (6 mm) long. Conventional wisdom might say that you should trim the wick first and then light it, but with an oil lamp, you actually light it first and trim it second. It's the way you "adjust" the wick, like you would on a kerosene lamp, but instead of rolling it back, you trim it back.

8. As the flame is burning, you can adjust the length of the wick by pulling out with tweezers or trimming back with scissors. The goal is to keep the flame low and steady. A tall flame is smoky and dangerous.

9. Keep the oil on your lamp topped up and it will continue to burn. Depending on how long you burn your lamp each day, you probably need to check the oil level and adjust the wick about once a day.

10. As with all open flames, only leave the oil lamp burning when you are at home and awake. You can snuff it out when you go to sleep or leave the house and relight it when you awaken or return.

Honey Jars

Honey jars, or sweetening jars, are an amazing mashup between food magic and candle magic. A honey jar spell is used to sweeten a particular person toward you. The vast majority of honey jars are used for lovers or lovers-to-be, but they can also be used to sweeten bosses, family members, neighbors, judges, clients, coworkers, or just about anyone you may come in contact with.

Because honey jars are ongoing spells, they are excellent for headstrong people and stubborn cases. They are ideal in situations where you have to wear someone down to be sweeter and kinder to you—for example, after a standoff with a lover who is stubbornly refusing to call you, a neighbor with a long-standing resentment toward you, or a boss who has always been a grump.

With honey jar spells, you take a honey jar that you have prepared magically and burn a small candle on top of it at regular intervals, either daily or on special days of the week. The work of a honey jar only ends when you get the result that you want. As you burn the candles over the days, weeks, and months, drips of wax will start to build up on the outside of the jar. This wax buildup is a positive sign of the energy that is building up around your intention, softening the other person's heart toward you, and sealing the love you have. The goal is to have a jar covered with wax drips built up over many, many days.

As your candles burn down on top of your honey jar, be sure to remove any leftover pieces of wick. These little black wick ends can build up, and too many of them in a clump can reignite and burn out of control.

I also recommend using a small jar and small candles for this kind of spell. Select a jar with a metal lid—plastic lids can catch fire, and nobody likes the smell of burning plastic. A small jar ensures quicker visible results of wax buildup, and if you are working your candle over days, weeks, and months, you'll see the wax on that little jar grow bigger and bigger.

Select a candle color that supports your intention (see the section on candle colors in chapter 2 for guidance). You can work different candle colors on different days. For example, on a love spell you might want to alternate between red for passion, pink for romance, and blue for reconciliation. The ideal candle is a chime candle or a slim taper, something that will burn in an hour or two. Another alternative is to burn a small votive candle freestanding, not inside a glass jar. Some people like to use larger candles, but those defeat the purpose of preparing and burning a candle each day. They might build up drippy wax quickly, but the point of a honey jar is to work on something over time and send your intention out over and over again; and too much wax too quickly doesn't offer that experience. Other people like to use tea lights, which are the right size but come in containers that prevent wax from dripping on the jar.

Working with a honey jar involves working with personal concerns. Personal concerns are personal items coming from your target. Personal concerns range from the most intimate to more distant. You can gauge the kind of personal concern that will work for you and your intentions by judging the level of intimacy of your relationship and choosing a personal concern that is the strongest that you can get. Here is a list of personal concerns you might use in a honey jar ranging from the ones with the strongest ties to the target to the weakest:

Personal Concerns

- Semen, vaginal fluid, or menstrual blood
- Blood, saliva, sweat, mucus, or urine
- Body hair or hair from the head
- Toenail clippings, fingernail clippings, or skin scrapings

- Clothing that has been worn by the target and not washed (the more intimate and closer to the body, the more powerful)
- Dirt from a footprint or foot track of your target
- Handwritten signature
- Something that was owned by the person
- Something touched by the person
- Photograph of the person

Select the personal concern that is the strongest one that you can get in the situation. For example, if you were doing a honey jar on a judge to get them to favor you in a court case, it would be highly unlikely that you would be able to get a fingernail clipping or piece of hair, but it is conceivable that you could get a signature. Likewise, if you are working on getting a lover to be sweeter toward you, just using a photo of them in your honey jar is a very weak link to them. Using a piece of hair or some body fluids will produce much better results.

 ## Honey Jar Spell

YOU WILL NEED

    Jar of honey with a metal lid

    Paper for petition

    Personal concern

    Small candles (slim tapers or chime candles)

    Spoon

    Pen or pencil

Herbs

Spiritual oil

1. Prepare a petition paper.

2. Drop a pinch of the herb mixture onto the petition paper.

3. Add your target's personal concern to your petition paper packet. If the spell is for love, it's traditional to tie a piece of your hair around your target's hair and add this as your personal concern.

4. Fold the petition paper toward you as you say your intention or prayer aloud. Turn the paper 90 degrees to the right and fold toward you again as you speak your wish. Continue to turn, speak, and fold until you can fold it no more.

5. Open the jar of honey, take a small spoonful of honey and eat it, saying "As this honey is sweet to me, so (name of person) will be sweet to me." Do this three times.

6. Insert the petition paper packet into the jar, pushing it down into the honey with the spoon and close the lid.

7. Dress one of your candles with an appropriate spiritual oil, applying it in an upward motion, from base to wick, if you are bringing something in, or downward from wick toward base, if you are clearing out something.

8. Apply a lit match to the bottom of the candle to soften it and stick it to the top of the jar lid. Light the candle, speaking your spell words one last time. Let the candle burn completely.

9. Depending on the speed needed or the intensity of your desire, you may burn one candle every Monday, Wednesday, and Friday *or* one candle each day of the week.

10. If there are any burnt wick ends left over after you burn your candle, you should remove them to avoid a fire.

11. Continue to burn candles on the lid of your honey jar until you receive the desired result.

12. If at any point you would like to add something to your honey jar (for example, you want to add an herb or a stronger personal concern) you may open up the jar and break the wax drips to do so. Just close the lid when you are done and resume burning the candles on your schedule.

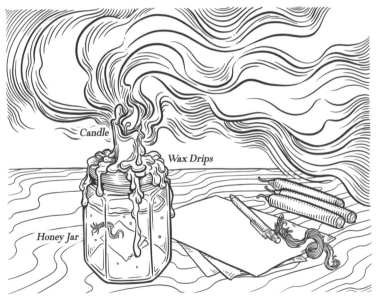

Candle

Wax Drips

Honey Jar

Honey Jar Spell

When you achieve your aims with a honey jar, don't dispose of it. A honey jar that has worked once can work again, and you may need to revisit that honey jar work if you and the other person have an argument or you need to improve the relationship in some way. If you have achieved your aims and you're done working on your honey jar, put it away in a safe place for possible use later. The only situation where I would recommend disposing of a honey jar is if you will never have contact with the person again; for example, you move away from your neighbor or you get a new job with a different boss.

Vinegar Jars

Vinegar jars are similar to honey jars in principle but are used for the opposite purpose—to sour someone's feelings. This is a negative working that is used to create rifts between people, break up alliances, or embitter one person toward another.

With vinegar jar spells, you take a prepared jar filled with various souring, anger-inducing, and negative herbs and liquids and burn a small black candle on top of it at regular intervals, either daily or on special days of the week. Like a honey jar, the work only ends when you get the result you want. The wax that builds up is a sign of the negative energy building up around your targets. As your candles burn down, be sure to remove any leftover pieces of wick to avoid an out-of-control fire.

As with a honey jar, select the strongest personal concern you can get in the situation. Once you have achieved your aims, discard the vinegar jar by dumping it in your target's trashcan, burying it on their property, dumping the contents of the vinegar jar at a crossroads close to your target's home and disposing of the glass in their trashcan, or, barring any of these options, throwing out the entire jar in a trashcan far from your home.

 Vinegar Jar Spell

YOU WILL NEED

Jar of vinegar with a metal lid

Paper for petition

Personal concern (see honey jars above for details on personal concerns)

Small candles (slim tapers or chime candles)

Spoon

Pen or pencil

Herbs

Spiritual oil

1. Prepare a petition paper.

2. Drop a pinch of the herb mixture onto the petition paper.

3. Add your targets' personal concerns.

4. Fold the petition paper away from you as you say your intention or prayer aloud. Turn the paper 90 degrees to the left and fold away from you again as you speak your wish. Continue to turn, speak, and fold until you can fold it no more.

5. Open the jar of vinegar and insert the packet into the jar, pushing it down into the vinegar, and close the lid.

6. Dress one of your candles with an appropriate spiritual oil, applying it from top to bottom, because you are banishing something.

7. Apply a lit match to the bottom of the candle to soften it and stick it to the top of the jar lid. Light the candle speaking your intention one last time. Let the candle burn completely.

8. Depending on the speed needed or the intensity of your desire, burn one candle every Tuesday, Thursday, and Saturday *or* one candle each day of the week.

9. If there are any burnt wick ends left over after you burn your candle, you should remove them to avoid a fire.

10. Continue to burn candles on the lid of your vinegar jar until you receive the desired result.

11. Depending on what you add to your vinegar jar, the contents sometimes start fermenting and pressure can build up inside. If the lid starts bulging out, you may slowly open up the jar and break the wax drips to do so. Just close the lid when you are done and resume burning the candles on schedule.

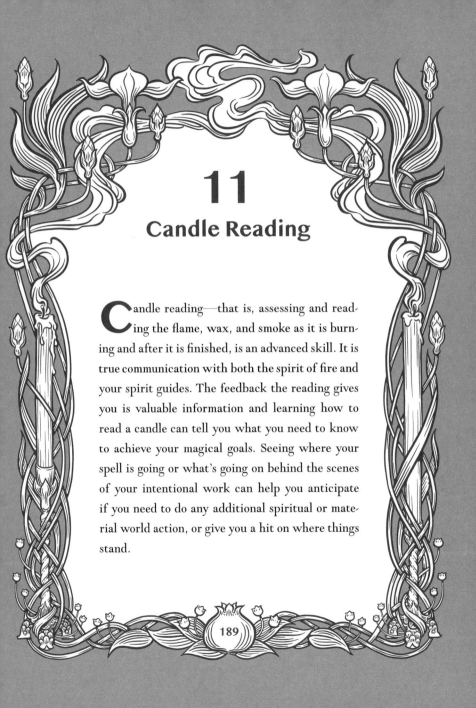

11
Candle Reading

Candle reading—that is, assessing and reading the flame, wax, and smoke as it is burning and after it is finished, is an advanced skill. It is true communication with both the spirit of fire and your spirit guides. The feedback the reading gives you is valuable information and learning how to read a candle can tell you what you need to know to achieve your magical goals. Seeing where your spell is going or what's going on behind the scenes of your intentional work can help you anticipate if you need to do any additional spiritual or material world action, or give you a hit on where things stand.

The three branches of candle reading are called ceromancy (wax reading), pyromancy (flame reading), and capnomancy (smoke reading). You are not required to master these skills to do a spell, but learning to do this interpretive work will enhance your magical ability.

One of the advantages to paying attention to your candle as it is burning is that you can head off any potential problems and effectively alter the direction of your magic. Because your candle is still burning, you have the opportunity to "work" the spell if something is going in a direction that you don't like. Candle flames that go out, flames that burn out of control, wax that spills over the sides of the tray—all of these can give information about what's going on while your spell is in motion.

For example, if you're doing a love spell and are seeing signs that indicate that your love will take some time to get going, then you can "work" the candle to give the situation some movement or do some additional magical work to help the situation along. Some people ask me if they have to watch the candle continually while it's burning. Unless you have unlimited time and a meditative nature, it's not really necessary to watch a candle the whole time that it's burning, but you do want to keep an eye on it. Ask any experienced candle burning spell caster and they will tell you stories of trays cracking, glass candle holders exploding, and things catching on fire. Keep yourself, your loved ones, and your property safe by keeping a burning candle within eyesight.

Working a candle while it is burning is a somewhat controversial approach in the magical community. There are many people who believe that once a candle is lit, you have to let it do what it's going to do and not interfere with it. In their opinion, if a candle goes out … well, it's a sign that you don't get what you want.

However, I believe in *spell work* with an emphasis on the *work*. To me, this is logical—magic is shifting or changing something to your will.

So why would you allow the candle to take control of your destiny? You are the one setting the course, you are the captain of your magical ship. So, if a candle does one of these odd things, take note of what it means but feel free to correct the course of your journey.

It is also great to read the wax after your candle has completed burning. One of the wonderful things about a candle spell is that it can give you feedback from the spirit realm as to what to expect from your working. The most common ways to interpret a candle once a spell is finished are to read the wax remains and to read soot or smoke on a glass encased candle.

Ceromancy or Wax Reading

Ceromancy is reading the wax remains while your candle is burning and after your candle is complete. The more experience you have, the more candles you have burned, the more aware you'll be of something that is out of the ordinary. When a candle burns in the usual way, the expectation is that the spell was successful and that you can count on seeing positive results from your work. And the definition of a "normal" burn depends on the kind of candle you are burning. Candles burned on trays or in candle holders have one way that they are interpreted, and candles burned in a glass container have another way that they are interpreted.

Ceromancy for Freestanding Candles on Trays or in Candle Holders

The default for a freestanding candle is that the wax burns down to the tray, all wax burns away or any leftover melted wax stays within the tray, is flat, and has no pieces left standing. When you see something other than this, then there is a message for you.

Reading Shapes and Symbols in the Wax

The most interesting way to read wax is to look for shapes and symbols in the wax remains. Just like looking for symbols in the clouds or tea leaf reading, you can practice and become quite intuitive in seeing images in the wax remains once a candle has finished burning.

Look for symbolic shapes in the wax and interpret their meaning as they relate to your spell. For example, you might be doing a spell for protection and see a silhouette of a profile. This shape can indicate a person being involved in the outcome of the spell, either living or as a spirit guide.

You can read the glitter and herbs that remain as well. Look for meaningful symbols and shapes in the flows of glitter or the herbs that are left behind in the wax.

Don't forget to examine the "negative space" (an art term for the space between and around a painted object) for symbols as well. Sometimes shapes and symbols in the space between flows of wax can show us deep unconscious or unknown information about our magical objective. Negative space shapes are always simple silhouettes (for example a heart shape) but can have profound implications in showing us what we don't know about the situation.

To hone your skills as a wax reader, start by looking for simple shapes. Squint your eyes slightly as you examine the wax from all angles and look for meaningful shapes in the flows of wax like you might look for shapes in the clouds. For more practice at this type of intuitive visualization, delve into learning the art of tea leaf reading and hone your gifts of interpretation. Check out appendix V for a list of basic symbols and their meanings and the bibliography for some helpful books on tea leaf reading with more extensive symbol dictionaries.

No Wax on the Tray

No wax on the tray indicates that your spell is going to move quickly toward your goal with no blocks or interference.

Excess Wax on Tray

Excess wax is a tricky one for freestanding candles; after all, most freestanding candles will leave *some* wax. I consider "excess wax" to refer to a candle that has not burned all the way down to the tray in the circle around the wick. When the candle hasn't burned completely, the reading indicates that there is some material world action that needs to be taken to reach the desired outcome. For example, if this was a spell for a raise, the practical action necessary might be asking the boss for the raise or putting in some extra hours.

Wax Flow and Drip Direction

Wax flow is another way the candle can speak to us. Wax can flow in all directions around the base of the candle, which is perfectly normal. If the wax flows or drips evenly in all directions, there is no need to take note of the direction. However, if all your wax flows or drips in only one direction or it generally flows evenly all around except for one long tendril of wax flowing in one direction, it may be a sign.

For the purposes of a candle reading, the top of the plate is north, the bottom is south, left is west, and right is east. These do not have to be the true direction, but just a direction that we attribute relative to the front of the candle spell tray. The direction indicates the areas where you need to put your attention and is one of the reasons I like to use square plates and trays for candle spells.

Witchy tip: When I do a candle layout, I make it a habit to put some talismans, gemstones, or larger roots in the front of the candle (in the direction of south) so that I always know the orientation of the candle even after the candle has burned all the way down. If I move the tray, I can still see the gemstones, roots, or talismans, identify which side of the tray is south, and therefore know the other directions and can interpret the wax flow.

Wax Flow in North, South, West, East Directions

East

Wax flowing to the right of the candle indicates new beginnings, mental work, and communication (written, spoken, with people, or with spirits). It also indicates that the outcome is ahead in the future, and how far it flows to the right indicates how far in the future you may expect your results. It can also indicate that brilliant new insights and

"Eureka!" moments will come to you that will help you to bring your spell to fruition.

South

Wax flowing toward you as the viewer or down in the direction of south would indicate passion, intensity, lust, action, will, and energy. It also means that the outcome will come to you quickly but that you may have to do some work to keep the results going. It can also indicate that a burst of action and energy will come to put your spell into motion.

West

Wax flowing to the left as you view the candle indicates spiritual matters, psychic awareness, dreams, the subconscious, divine connections, spirit guides, angels, saints, deities, and the supernatural. It also indicates that the outcome has connections to the past, and healing or dealing with the past will assist with reaching your magical objective. It can also mean that spiritual help is on the way or that a cleansing of the situation is occurring.

North

Wax flowing away from you as you face the candle or in the direction of north indicates material world issues, physicality, objects, places, the body, money, prosperity, and property. It indicates that the outcome will be positively influenced by practicality. It can also indicate the the objective may take some time to manifest but that the results will be long lasting.

Wax directions can also have gradations that incorporate more than one direction. If wax flows northwest (in between north and west), it can be said that the message incorporates elements of both north and west and, depending on the closeness to one direction or the other, it can indicate a greater influence of that direction.

Wax Pillars

Drips of wax or slender slivers of wax that remain standing after the candle has burned are an indication of resistance or blockages. How these pillars look at the end of the spell working can tell a lot. If the pillars are tall relative to the original height of the candle, they can indicate large and long-standing blocks. Small pillars indicate small and surmountable blocks. If the pillars are standing when the candle is complete, it indicates that the blocks are still in place. If the pillars have fallen down, the blocks were there but have been removed through the spell work.

When your candle work is done, pay attention to the pillars that have fallen and the ones still standing. If you look closely at the position of these pillars, you can get some hints as to what blocks have been removed and which ones you still have to work on. First, look at the quadrant they are standing in. For example, if a pillar has fallen on the "east" side of your tray, you are getting a message that mental blocks have been cleared away. Or if you see a pillar still standing in the "south," that indicates that there are blocks that need to be worked on in regards to passion or action.

You can also look at where the pillars are in relation to other candles. If a pillar is standing between two candles, it can mean there is a block between what those two candles represent. If there is a fallen pillar between them, then the blocks that were once there have been knocked down.

If you are working with candles of different colors in your spell, taking note of which color pillar is standing or has fallen and looking up the meanings of different colors as described in chapter 2 can also give you information as to where the blocks have been removed or where they still need to be worked on.

Wax Pillars

Candle Falls Over

If your candle falls over on its own, first check to see that you had affixed it correctly to the candle holder or tray and that it wasn't too close to another candle or other heat source that softened the candle. A candle that wasn't inserted firmly into a holder and falls over can simply indicate that you need to take more care when setting up your candle. If a candle that was set up securely falls over, I think of it like someone knocking on your door. It indicates that you need to pay attention to something regarding the topic of your spell. It may be that your spirit guides are trying to get your attention and you're missing an important message. Put the candle back upright, light it again, and look for messages out in the world regarding your spell topic. If your candle keeps falling over, the spirits may be telling you, "Try a different spell for this issue."

Glass Holder or Ceramic Tray Breaks or Explodes

A candle that is loaded with too many leafy or petal-y dried herbs can create a dangerous fire that heats up to the point that it cracks a tray or glass or can even make a glass jar explode. Of course, you can avoid this by being minimalistic in your application of any flammable "extras" like herbs or petition papers.

However, if a candle that has been dressed with a minimal amount of herbs and oils cracks a glass or tray, that indicates someone is working against you having your good outcome. Do a cleansing candle spell (such as an Energetic Purification vigil candle) and a protection spell (a Powerful Protection vigil candle is great for this) and then do a second round of your original candle spell. However, if the goal of your spell is banishing, reversing, or separation and your candle glass or plate breaks, this is a sign that the person or energy has been cast out or the ties between the parties involved will be broken apart in a spectacular way.

Candle Tunneling

When candles burn down the center only with a crater or "shell" of the original candle remaining, it's called "tunneling." Many large decorative pillar candles are designed to tunnel, so that you'll see the glow of the flame through the sides of the pillar as the center burns down. Unintentional tunneling happens when the wick is too slender or is the wrong type for the candle. If your candle was designed to burn completely and you have burned other candles by the same maker and have not had an issue with tunneling, you can be sure that it is a sign.

Candle Burning on One Side and Tunneling

Tunneling indicates that a wall is up or that there is unfinished business in this area. You can figure out in what area these walls exist by seeing what parts of the candle remain. The front of a figural candle means that there are blocks facing out to the world, the back of a figural candle means that there are subconscious blocks. I also look to see if there are symbolic areas of the candle that remain intact. For example, if I burn a skull candle and the mouth remains, I see that as a sign that walls are up around communication. If the back of the skull is still intact and standing upright, then there are things in the back of the target's mind that are preventing openness. If the tunneling is higher on one side, you can also observe if the higher part faces a direction (north, south, east, or west) and read this as resistance being higher around these areas.

Candle Burns on One Side Only

If your candle burns on one side only, it could be because of a draft blowing the flame to one side, poor wick placement, or the candle maker using the wrong size wick. If none of these are the case, look to the direction (north, south, east, or west) the candle remains are standing to see the unfinished business, resistance, or block.

Wax Spills over the Side of Holder or Tray

If the wax of your candle spills over the side of your tray or dish, it could simply be a case of having a dish that is too small to contain the wax. However, if the tray is of an appropriate size and you see unusual flows of wax over the side of the tray or dish, this could indicate an excess of expression of some kind; the advice is to keep more of your words, ideas, or emotions to yourself to assist in your spell outcome. Also look to see what direction this wax is flowing (north, south, east, or west) as this may give you some insights.

Ceromancy for Candles in Glass Containers

When it comes to ceromancy, candles in glass containers have fewer elements to read compared to candles burned on trays. With glass-encased candles, the wax reading is generally simpler: either the wax burned completely or it didn't. It's also possible to read any remaining wax, along with herbs and glitter, to discern more symbolic messages about your spell.

No Wax in the Bottom of the Glass

An ideal burn for a glass contained candle is for the wax to burn completely. Wax that has burned completely indicates that there is no extra material world work or effort that has to be done on your part and that your spell work is going to help things move quickly toward your goal with no problems.

Wax on Bottom or Side of Glass

When there is wax left over in the bottom or on the side of a glass-encased candle, it indicates that there is material world action that needs to be taken to see the desired result. For example, if there is excess wax in a Steady Work candle, you may have to fill out more applications or revise your resume. The more wax that remains, the more action and effort necessary.

Reading Shapes and Symbols on the Glass

It is also possible to read symbols in the remains of a glass-encased candle. Wax, herbs, glitter, and soot can all leave shapes that can be interpreted just like reading tea leaves in a tea cup. Be sure to look for shapes in the remains and in any blank spaces between the remains. When you discern these shapes, you can look up their symbolic meaning in a list of spiritual symbols. You can find a list of typical symbols in appendix V or look up symbolic meanings in a dream dictionary or tea leaf reading book.

Pyromancy or Flame Reading

Pyromancy is the interpretation of fire, and in the case of candle magic, specifically the candle's flame. Reading the flame can be quite a mystical experience. One very old way to read a candle flame is to get into a trance state while staring at it in a darkened room. If you give yourself time to get into a trance, you will begin to see images in the candle flame and then you can interpret those images using a list of symbols like the one found in appendix V.

Whenever you are reading the flame, it's important to be aware of the effects of drafts on your candle. Drafts from doors, windows, vents, air conditioners, and heaters can make a flame move or cause it to burn only one side of a candle. If you notice an unusual flame, move your candle to another room or another part of the room to see if the flame continues to behave in the same way. You can also light another candle and place it near your original candle to observe if both candles are burning the same or differently.

Candle Flame Burns Even and Steady

The positive default for a candle flame is a strong and steady flame. Ideally, your flame should be about ½" (12 mm) tall and burn at an even rate, and the flame itself should be calm and steady. A flame that burns in this ideal way indicates positive results for your spell.

Candle Flame Burns High

When we note a candle flame burning too high, it's a sign that emotions are running hot or the situation feels out of control. Trimming the wick and getting the flame to return to a normal height is an act of willfully "turning down the heat" in the situation, that is, recognizing that something is getting out of hand and knowing that you have the ability to bring things back under control.

A right-sized flame should be about ½" (12 mm) tall. If your candle flame is burning too high, snuff the candle, trim the wick with a wick trimmer or scissors to about ¼" (6 mm) and relight it. A wick that is about ¼" (6 mm) long should get your flame back under control. Flames that burn too high will also create soot on the side of a glass jar or a vigil candle glass and give a false negative reading.

If working with a specific spirit, deity, or ancestor, a flame that suddenly shoots up high can indicate that they are present and around you.

Candle Burns Really Fast

If a candle flame is burning high, it is likely that the candle is also burning very fast. Candles that burn fast can represent a situation that is moving too fast. While some people might desire a quick result, quick resolutions indicated by a fast burn may produce results that are not very long lasting. You can remedy the spell by trimming the wick to ¼" (6 mm). Fast-burning candles can also present a problem if you are burning two candles that you want to burn at the same rate. For example, if you are burning two figural candles for love, it is best if they keep pace with each other. First, I would recommend that if you are burning two candles to represent two lovers, start with candles made by the same manufacturer so they are more likely to burn at the same rate. If one is burning dramatically faster than the other, you can snuff it out sooner and let the slower one catch up. In a case like this where one candle represents one person and another a different person, it would indicate that one person is likely to have hotter emotions and may be more likely to make hasty decisions or burn out in the relationship than the other. Trim the wick of the fast burning candle; when you relight it, check to see that it doesn't continue burning too quickly.

Candle Flame Is Weak

A weak candle flame indicates that there is not enough pure energy or will focused in the direction of the spell. Oftentimes, a weak flame is a reflection of wishy-washy intentions, such as "I want that new car, but how will I be able to afford it?"

For spiritualists and ghost hunters, a flame that suddenly drops down low can indicate that spirits are in the room. Taking a candle from room to room and watching to see if the flame dims is an old-fashioned way of checking for the presence of ghosts in particular areas of a house.

Candle Flame Alternates between Strong and Weak

A candle that alternates between a bright, strong flame and a low, weak flame indicates moodiness, inconsistent feelings, cycles of low and high motivation, or a tendency toward hot and cold emotions.

Candle Burns Really Slowly

Just as a candle can burn too quickly, it's also possible that it can burn too slowly. Unless you are burning more than one of the same candle at the same time or have burned many candles of the same type, it may be difficult to tell whether a candle is burning slower than usual. One of the most noticeable ways to spot a slow burn is a candle that seems to have burned all the way down to the bottom of the glass jar or tray but keeps burning and burning ... and burning. If you do notice a slow burn, it indicates that the spell might take longer than usual to produce results. On the other hand, it can also signify that once results are achieved, they will be long-lasting and productive for an extended time.

Candle Flame Goes Out

If your candle flame goes out but the wick is still upright and visible, first check to see if there is a draft that may have blown the candle out or if someone in the home extinguished the candle without telling you. If you can rule out these natural causes or you are unsure, relight the candle. If it goes out again, it is the Universe telling you "not now." If you light it a total of three times and it goes out each time, the answer to your spell objective is a definite "no." Don't despair. Start a new spell with a reframed objective. For example, if you were doing a spell to get John Smith to fall in love with you and the flame went out on its own three times, start a new spell inviting in your perfect partner without specifying that it's John Smith. This "no" may be the Universe's way of telling you that there is someone much better for you out there.

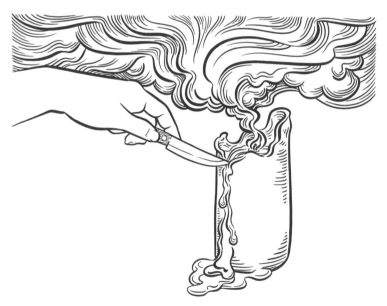

Cutting Channels in Side of Candle

Candle Flame Drowns in the Wax

Candle flames can "drown" in wax; that is, the wick can go out because there is too much wax pooling up and it puts out the flame. Spiritually, a candle drowning can indicate that there isn't enough fire, passion, or motivation about the issue or that someone is drowning in their sad emotions.

On the practical level, this happens when a candle is tunneling or has a wick that's too small for the candle diameter. If you have the experience of a candle "drowning," you can burn an identical candle to see if it's an issue with the candle manufacturing.

If your freestanding pillar or figural candle is drowning, I recommend cutting channels in the side of the tunneling candle to allow the wax to flow out onto your tray or pouring out the excess wax.

Wick Disappears

There are times when a candle wick seems to disappear completely before the candle is complete. If your candle goes out before it reaches the bottom and there is no wick to be seen, it could be an error in the candle manufacture or it could be a severely drowned wick.

A disappearing wick indicates some extreme sluggishness around your magical intention and a need for more passion, enthusiasm, energy, or action. It is resistance, but resistance through malaise, indifference, or laziness rather than actively fighting against an outcome.

When this happens, the solution is to assist the candle burn by adding a new helper wick. Drill or gouge a small hole in the center of the candle using an awl, metal chopstick, or metal knitting needle, and insert a small piece of wick (now is when you can use the little saved wick pieces that were trimmed from new candles before lighting them for the first time). The new wick only needs to extend out of the candle about ¼" (6 mm); if you can extend it into the candle at least ¼" (6 mm), you will have enough to relight the candle. Once the candle starts burning again, you can use a candle tool to dig through the melted wax pool and see if you can find the original wick. Sometimes the original wick makes an appearance after adding the helper wick. The original wick can even spontaneously light up again. If it does, it can create a double flame, but this should not necessarily be interpreted symbolically—it is merely caused by the two wicks in the candle.

Adding a New Wick

Something Catches Fire

Another thing that commonly happens with spells is that something besides the wick catches fire, which is *the* reason I emphasize safety with any candle magic. You must be available to put out any things that may catch fire—being awake and at home is essential to safety.

Herbs can catch on fire, petition papers can get lit (not in the good-time way), and even the tiny bits of black wick that accumulate at the bottom of a vigil candle or on a honey jar can burst into crazy flames.

First things first: if something is burning out of control, snuff it out. If it's really burning out of control, use a fire extinguisher! Assess the issue. Was there a real-world reason your candle was burning like crazy? I have purchased some gorgeous fixed candles from amazing practitioners I respect and admire that were lovingly piled with herbs and oils on top of herbs and oils, like a seven-layer dip. While this may appear social media ready, it makes for problems when the candle burns and all that's left are flammable materials. Did you write a novel-sized petition paper and place it directly under your candle? You *might* want to place that novel under the tray instead of the candle next time. Look at the practical causes for why your spell caught fire. If it was because you were overenthusiastic in adding flammable elements to your candle spell, chalk it up to learning and do the candle spell over again in a more restrained and subdued way.

If there is no apparent mundane reason your candle turned into a conflagration, then you've got a spiritual message that you can look at. Fires that burn out of control represent an issue that is out of control. Are there high emotions? Anger? Destructive feelings? Do you need to "burn through" something before you manifest your good outcome? I would recommend doing the spell again with a more grounded kind of magic. Do a cleansing spell before redoing your spell and incorporate gemstones and roots (both are very grounding) into your magic.

"Knots" in the Wick

Bulbous looking black bumps in the wick as the candle burns are called "knots," as they look like the wick has been tied in a knot or like the knot on the branch of a tree. These mushroom-like bulges are the result of carbon building up on the wick as it burns. As they occur, they should be trimmed with a wick trimmer or a pair of scissors. In glass-encased candles, these carbon knots can cause soot and smoke and lead to unnecessary negative interpretations in a candle reading.

Spiritually, knots in the wick indicate that something is "tied up" with your spell intention and may prevent your desired outcome unless you work to untie it. Usually I have found that these are thoughts or beliefs we have about the working. For example, if you burn a candle for a new love, a new job, or a new house but your wick keeps forming knots as you burn it, check your own thoughts or beliefs about your ability to attract this love/job/house to you and do the work to eliminate any inhibiting thoughts.

Talking Flames

Talking flames are one of my favorite flame readings. A talking flame is a flame that makes noises—chattering, popping, crackling, or hissing. A skilled candle reader with the gift of clairaudience (hearing messages from spirit guides or Spirit) can even go into a trance and translate the messages from Spirit regarding your spell.

Sometimes this chatter can come from herbs, like juniper berries, that pop when they are burned, or from a poorly made candle that had droplets of water mixed with the wax during the manufacturing process. If you're working with herbs you have burned before and a well-made candle, it's time to pay attention. Even a novice candle reader can interpret the level of talk and what it can indicate.

Soft and Infrequent Chatter

Secret messages, intimate conversation, pure thoughts, gentle loving words from your guides or your target.

Mild but Frequent Chatter

Important messages, divine directives, copious information, your guides or your target having a lot to communicate to you.

Loud, Frequent Pops and Crackles

Disagreements, arguments, stern warnings, your guides or your target saying, "Pay attention!"

When you get audible messages, look at the other signs in your candle reading to determine what the message is about; more importantly, listen to corroborating messages out in the world and see what Spirit is trying to tell you.

Flickering Flame

A flickering, jumping, or dancing flame (without a draft to cause it) is an indication of spirit guides encouraging and influencing the spell positively. The same applies to spells done on yourself. If your flame is dancing, the changes you want are already starting to happen. If the movement is intense or erratic, it could indicate that the road to get to the result might be a tad chaotic.

Double Flame

Double flames can be caused by knots in the wick breaking off, an added helper wick and an original wick burning at the same time, or sprinkled herbs catching fire. If the double flame is not a result of these real-world sources, it can indicate a separation, division, or two separate sources or points of attraction   for the work you're doing. If you are working on a target, that person is sending the same energy back to you. It can also indicate that a "twin flame" issue is at play; you may need to do some additional spell work to bring the two entities together. If the candle spell is for a reunion or reconciliation, two flames may indicate a temporary or permanent separation. See if the flames join up again (or help them to join up again) to encourage the pair to come together.

Colored Flames

Colored flames other than yellow and orange are usually the result of some additional material in the candle that creates colors when burned. However, colored flames that do not have a physical source are quite magical and are a message from Spirit about the nature of your spell. Look up the meaning of the color and interpret what it means in terms of your spell work.

Sparking

Candle sparks can happen when flammable material is in the wax pool. Things such as burned wicks and match ends can create sparks, which can be dangerous if they catch something on fire (yet another great reason to keep a burning candle within sight). A candle that sparks, without these extra flammable materials, is an indicator that flashes of intuitive insight will bring solutions to the problems at hand.

Flame Won't Go Out

If you attempt to snuff out your candle multiple times and it doesn't go out, you have a candle that doesn't want to be extinguished. A candle that resists being extinguished is telling you that you're not done with your work. See if there is some additional magical work that you can add to support your intention. Maybe it's doing a cleansing bath, carrying a charm bag, or adding to your petition. Do some divination work (for example, getting a reading or working with a pendulum) to help you to figure out what additional spiritual work is needed.

Flames Bending Away or Together

If a flame is bending, first check to see if there is a draft in the room by moving the candle or looking at other candles around the bent one. A flame of one candle bending away from another candle indicates that the energy of one candle wants to "run away" from the other. If the flame of one leans toward another, it indicates attraction.

In cases where the candles represent people, this can mean the feelings of the person are moving toward or away from the objective or the other person. If the candles are representative of separate intentions (for example, a candle for prosperity and a candle for success), they may be incompatible with each other (if bending away) or need to be brought together in a more sincere way (if bending toward one another).

Candle Flame Bending in a Certain Direction

In the case of reading candle flames bending in a certain direction, I personally tend to read them only in the true compass directions (not left, right, top, or bottom of the tray). When you see a candle flame leaning in one direction and there is no draft, take out a compass to understand what your spirit guides are trying to tell you.

East

A candle flame leaning to the east indicates inspired ideas and verbal or written messages coming to you to help achieve your outcome. If the spell is done on another person, it can mean that they are thinking of you.

South

A flame that leans south indicates that passionate actions and optimistic energy will lead you in the right direction. Fires of passion are burning and can be harnessed for a good outcome.

West

A flame that bends toward the west tells you to trust the spiritual assistance and synchronicities that will flow to you. Gentle emotion and intuition are the correct senses to rely on for best results.

North

A flame bending toward the north is a sign to take advantage of practical opportunities that will present themselves. Results will move toward you at a slow and steady pace and concrete manifestations will be seen.

Capnomancy or Smoke Reading

Capnomancy is the art of smoke reading and can be done as a candle is burning or, in the case of glass-encased candles, after the candle is extinguished. The ideal candle should give off little to no smoke as it burns. Excess smoke can indicate a poorly made candle; a candle with too many herbs, oils, or other adulterants added; or a wick that needs trimming because it is too long or has built-up carbon.

If you have addressed any mundane causes and are still seeing smoke, it is time to do some capnomancy. One of the more mystical ways of doing a smoke reading is to induce a trance state and watch the smoke as it curls to divine symbolic images and interpret what those symbols mean, but there are plenty of other ways to do smoke readings that don't require this level of skill.

Candle Smoke Direction

While a candle is burning, check to see the direction that the smoke is flowing. Like a candle flame, smoke drifting in a certain direction can indicate a draft in the room. But if there is no draft, pay attention to the direction in which the smoke drifts. Use a compass to determine the smoke's direction.

East

Smoke drifting to the east will indicate that using logic in the situation will bring the best outcomes and that positive results are ahead in the future.

South

Smoke that drifts south indicates that it is time to take creative action to achieve your goals and that you are attracting something into your life.

West

Smoke that flows west means that prayer, meditation, or spiritual work around the topic will produce the strongest results; additionally, revising, reworking, or fixing something from the past will help you attain your objective.

North

Smoke drifting toward the north would indicate that diligent, practical step-by-step working toward your goal will help you to achieve your aims and that clearing away some negativity is necessary for success.

Reading Soot

Smoke residue on glass-encased candles can also be read as they burn or after they are finished. Before assessing whether the soot has a spiritual meaning, check to see that you are not allowing the soot to build up unchecked. Smoke often comes from poorly made candles with cheap fragrances, inappropriate wicks, or adulterated wax. It can also result from wicks that have built up carbon or have not been trimmed. More often than not, it shows up from candles that have been dressed with too much oil, fragrance, or herb pieces. Make sure that you have been tending your candle all along before you throw up your hands and say, "Soot happens!" Soot that shows up despite your best efforts to keep these factors in check indicates spiritual issues surrounding your spell.

Dark black soot that blocks the candlelight through the glass indicates spiritual blockages around your intention. The density of the soot indicates the level of blockage—a dark grey haze that still allows light to come through indicates small, annoying blockages that can be overcome, while thick, dense, black soot that won't allow light through indicates heavy blockages that may need some additional cleansing work.

A glass that shows soot is not a cause for despair. If the glass clears up as you look down the sides of the glass, it means that the blockages can be cleared. The length of the soot on the glass indicates how long you will have to work on clearing the blockage. For example, a candle glass with black soot an inch (2 cm) down the rim indicates that the issue can be resolved pretty quickly with some spiritual cleansing work. A dense soot that goes all the way down to nearly the bottom of the glass would indicate that you may have to work at clearing up a spiritually blocked situation for a while before things start moving forward. A candle that burns black from top to bottom is a hard "no" from the Universe, so try approaching the problem from a different angle or do a different kind of spell. For example, instead of doing a reconciliation spell, do a spell to find a new (and even better) love, or do some focused spiritual cleansing work to remove all that negative spiritual gunk.

Isolated spots of dense soot on the side of a candle glass indicate beliefs you hold that are preventing you from achieving your outcome. Self-judgment, lack of confidence, or a feeling of unworthiness may be hindering the spell work. The size of the spot will indicate how big a problem these internalized feelings and beliefs are.

If the soot on your candle jar is dense, some action in the spiritual realm is necessary. There are a couple of options: do your spell over again from scratch, which may be all that is necessary for minor blocks. For bigger blocks or longstanding issues, it may be worthwhile to first burn an Energetic Purification, Block Buster, Open Roads, or Van Van candle to remove spiritual blocks, and, when this cleansing candle has burned cleanly and completely, light another candle for your original intention.

Additionally, you may want to do another kind of cleansing to enhance your work. Doing a series of three, seven, nine, or thirteen cleansing baths with either prepared bath crystals or epsom salt and sea salt plus a few drops of the appropriate spiritual oil can remove blocks surrounding you—this cleansing is also particularly good for internal-ized negative beliefs.

Sometimes pale grey or white soot will appear on a candle glass and that indicates that your spirit guides are surrounding you on this issue and would like to help you with your situation. If you don't cur-rently have a connection to your spirit guides, connect with your guides through prayer, meditation, a session with a medium, or setting up a spirit guide altar. Ask for assistance and see what they have to say about your situation.

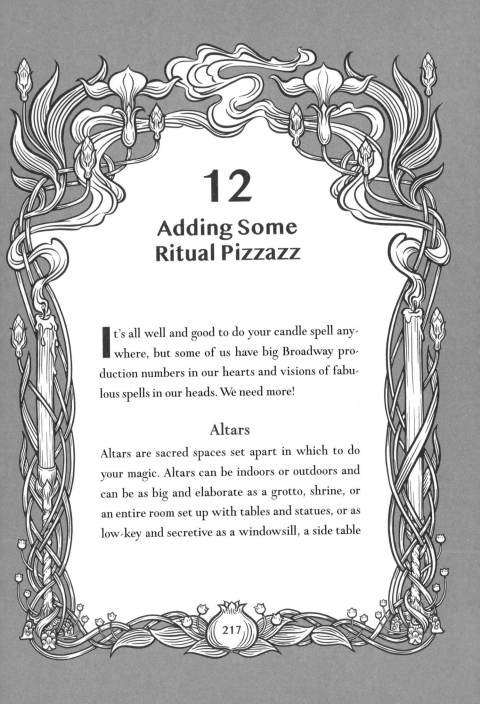

12

Adding Some Ritual Pizzazz

It's all well and good to do your candle spell anywhere, but some of us have big Broadway production numbers in our hearts and visions of fabulous spells in our heads. We need more!

Altars

Altars are sacred spaces set apart in which to do your magic. Altars can be indoors or outdoors and can be as big and elaborate as a grotto, shrine, or an entire room set up with tables and statues, or as low-key and secretive as a windowsill, a side table or a shelf. One is not better than the other, it is simply a matter of what is practical and what pleases you.

The reason we set up an altar is to set aside a space to do our magical work. Just like a desk is a space set aside for writing or homework, setting up an altar draws our attention to our spell work. While it is entirely possible to do a candle spell and set it on our kitchen table (and when doing work on the down-low, it's actually to our benefit to make it fit in with the mundane parts of our space), creating an altar allows us to add many more supportive magical elements to our spell work.

If you have the option, choose a room where the magic will be most effective. Bedrooms are excellent for love and fertility spells, kitchens for family and prosperity work, bathrooms for cleansing and clearing spells, and living rooms for ancestor work, for example.

The main concern when setting up an altar for candle work is to keep it flameproof. Festooning your altar with cascading fabric, setting up a candle altar among colorful fall leaves, or scattering loose papers and pictures around a side table altar may look lovely, but is dangerous when they catch fire.

The ideal altar is made of stone or ceramic tile. Stone and tile are sturdy, non-flammable and do not conduct heat like metal does. A piece of granite or marble or a tile trivet placed on a tabletop can protect your altar from candles catching things on fire, is much easier to clean up than an altar cloth, and keeps a wood finish from stains or burns.

Placing statues, figurines, and framed pictures on altars can add beautiful elements and connect your work to deities, ancestors, spirit animals, angels, or other important spirits.

Valuable talismans can also be placed on your altar next to your candle spells rather than on your candle spell trays, so they won't get covered with wax and have to be cleaned. See appendix IV for examples of talismans.

Gemstones and crystals can be placed on altars to be blessed and can bring additional energies and support to your spell work. See appendix II for examples of some gemstones and their magical uses.

Offerings to goddesses, gods, ancestors, saints, angels, spirits, and elementals can also be placed on the altar to invite them to support your work. Alcohol, fruit, flowers, candies, tobacco, bread, cakes, and money are all examples of offerings left to spirits.

Natural items such as feathers, shells, rocks, pinecones, acorns, and branches can also be added to empower your spells. Make sure flammable items are placed at a safe distance from your candles. See appendix III for examples of shells and their magical uses and appendix IV for examples of natural talismans.

Ceremonial or magical items such as chalices, incense burners, bells, wands, athames, cauldrons, or mortars and pestles can be added to the altar and charged with the spirit energy of your spell or used to empower your spell.

Tools for doing your work at the altar such as matches, snuffers, carving tools, oils, your grimoire, and incense can be stored on or near your altar to empower these tools with magic as they wait to be used. They can be set on the altar as is or placed in attractive containers for easy access and to enhance the beauty of your altar.

Water elements such as a glass of spring water or a small table fountain can be added to your altar to invite spirit help and the energies of the element of water.

An altar cloth can be placed on the table under your stone slab to designate the space as sacred and separate from your mundane room. If you place an altar cloth on your tabletop, place your candle on a trivet or tile to keep it away from the altar cloth.

When creating an altar space, you can arrange things according to whatever pleases your eye or you can make a formal setting following the dictates of your personal spiritual path.

Altars can be set up in many places in the home or workplace. For example, a side table, console, fireplace mantel, windowsill (make sure there are no curtains to catch fire), nightstand, or the top of a dresser can be set up as an altar in your house. If you are allowed to burn candles at work, the corner of a desk or the top of a filing cabinet can serve as an altar space. Think creatively about spaces that can be set up as altars and you will find many options where you live and work.

Ritual

Ritual is an important part of a spiritual life—it allows us to leave the mundane world and enter into altered states where we can connect with spirit. In this place, magic becomes possible and our spells get an extra charge. Ritual allows us to let our minds go to other places, and spiritual rituals in particular let us get into the liminal states where we can most effectively change things on the spiritual realm.

One of the great gifts of having a religious practice is that all religions include an element of ritual. Even non-religious people have rituals. Family traditions, parades on special holidays, birthday cakes, greetings and good-byes—all of these incorporate some element of ritual.

The important part of ritual is that after repeating it over and over, at a certain point you'll no longer have to think about the steps. A mundane comparison would be the ability to automatically shake someone's hand when you are introduced in a business setting, which lets your mind focus on other things (like remembering their name!).

If you already have a spiritual path, you may already have some rituals (such as prayers) that you can incorporate into your candle spells, or you may have candle rituals that you can adapt to your magic. I encourage you to come up with rituals that work for you. You can most certainly light a candle for a spell without a ritual and still see good results, but if you really want to get into the space where the magic happens, try some rituals in your candle magic practice; see what works and what doesn't, and keep the things that make your magic sing.

To make a good ritual, you need a beginning, a middle, and an end. The preparation is a signal that you are stepping out of the mundane world and entering into the space where your focus is on your magic. The middle is where the magic takes place, and the closing signifies moving out of sacred space and back into the real world. Below are some examples of things that you can incorporate in your candle spell ritual:

Ritual Preparation

- Fasting or altering diet
- Gathering tools
- Preparing and arranging your altar
- Adorning yourself
- Cleansing yourself
- Cleansing your space (incense or spray)
- Playing music (recorded music or playing an instrument)
- Movement (dance, meaningful gestures, yoga)
- Meditation (silent meditation or guided meditation)

ADDING SOME RITUAL PIZZAZZ

- Writing your spell plan
- Free-writing your spell intention

Ritual Middles

- Inviting in the elements, spirits, deities, ancestors
- Prayer
- Chanting
- Singing
- Meditation
- Casting a circle
- Holding and charging your candle
- Putting your candle spell together
- Speaking your spell words (speaking, whispering, shouting, singing)
- Lighting your candle

Ritual Closings

- Words of closure ("it is done," "so mote it be," "amen")
- Thanking and releasing elements, spirits, deities, ancestors
- Grounding movement (touching the earth, lying down on the floor)
- Grounding visualizations (imagining your energy going back into the earth)
- Grounding action (eating or drinking something healthy)
- Putting away tools

Rituals can be as simple or as complex as whatever works for you. Below I give you an example of what I do when I do a full-blown candle lighting ritual at home for myself.

Ritual for Personal Prosperity

1. Put on meditative music that helps to define that I am about to do some spell work.

2. Take a cleansing bath using prepared Abundant Prosperity bath crystals or epsom salt, sea salt, and chamomile.

3. Put Magnetic Attraction oil on my body in an upward motion (from feet toward head).

4. Dress in clean clothes of green fabric.

5. Burn money drawing incense in the room where the altar is; for example, patchouli and benzoin on a bamboo charcoal. Alternatively, mix a few drops of Abundant Prosperity oil with spring water in a spray bottle, shake it up and spray around the room.

6. Prepare and set up my altar space, arranging lucky coins, special talismans, statues of the goddess Lakshmi and Fortuna (goddesses of prosperity and luck), and a petition paper with my intention on it.

7. Hold a green cat candle in my hands, close my eyes, and visualize my prosperity as I put my energy into the candle.

8. Put the candle on a tray, dressed with Abundant Prosperity oil, surrounded by yellow support candles, blue flag root, allspice berries, patchouli, calendula, and Job's tears.

9. Close my eyes and visualize my good outcome.

10. Ask for the aid of my spirit guides.

11. Speak my spell words and light the candle.

12. Close my eyes and again visualize my good outcome.

13. Thank my spirit guides and say "It is done."

14. Bend down and touch the floor with my fingertips to ground my energy.

15. Eat a bite of food to bring me back into the material realm.

Try planning out a ritual before doing your spell work. You can imagine scripting it like you would a show with a first, second, and third act. Decide what you'd like to incorporate and write down the steps on a piece of paper, so you don't have to worry about what comes next.

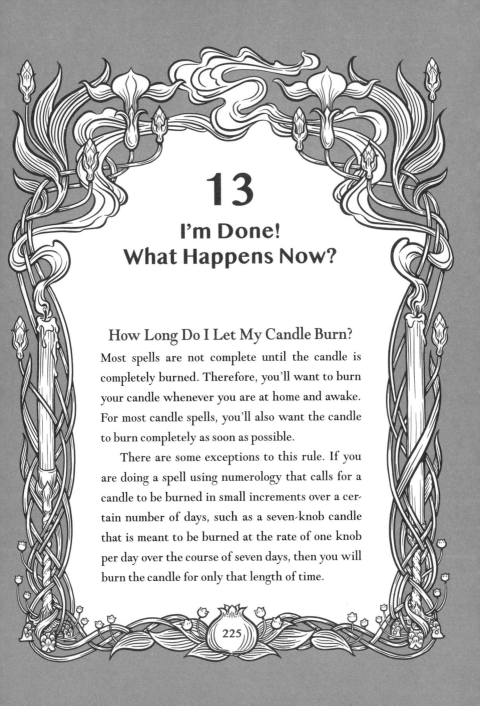

13
I'm Done! What Happens Now?

How Long Do I Let My Candle Burn?

Most spells are not complete until the candle is completely burned. Therefore, you'll want to burn your candle whenever you are at home and awake. For most candle spells, you'll also want the candle to burn completely as soon as possible.

There are some exceptions to this rule. If you are doing a spell using numerology that calls for a candle to be burned in small increments over a certain number of days, such as a seven-knob candle that is meant to be burned at the rate of one knob per day over the course of seven days, then you will burn the candle for only that length of time.

If you are going to burn your candle for more than three or four hours at a time, then you will need to trim the wick so that it doesn't get too hot, and trim the knots off the wick as it goes along to prevent the flame from getting too big and smoky.

In any case, once your candle has burned completely, your spell work is complete. Your work now is to envision, expect, and receive the positive results.

What to Do with Your Candle Remains

What do you do with your candle spell when it's complete? If you've burned a simple candle completely and there are no remains, there is nothing more to do. But with most candle spells, there is something left over at the end. There are many options for what may be done with these remains; your choice may depend on your spell work.

The Simple Way

The simplest way of disposing leftover candle wax is to throw it in the trash. While not terribly ceremonial, it does the trick; fancier disposals may not be necessary for simple spells. Throw it in your own trash if the spell was to bring something to you or a trashcan far from your home if you were doing uncrossing, banishing, or trying to clear something negative.

Keeping the Candle Remains

If you have been working with an invoking candle, you may take the remains off the tray or dish and place them in a paper bag or wrap them in a cloth and place them in an appropriate place (such as your bedroom for a love spell or your office for a prosperity spell) until your spell comes to fruition. When you get your wish, you can dispose of these remains in whatever manner you choose.

Alternatively, you can keep the energy of the spell ongoing by burying the wax and herb remains on your property or in a potted plant. Bury remains in your front yard if you are working to bring something to you, or in your backyard if you are wanting to keep something you already have.

Recycle Your Candle Holder

When your candle has completely burned down, you may choose to recycle the glass container. You will naturally want to reuse trays, dishes, and candle holders. If so, you need to take any remaining wax out of them. First, make sure your holder is oven safe (no plastic or anything that can melt), then place it on a pie plate or cake pan in an oven set at the very lowest setting (usually warm or between 150° and 170° Fahrenheit or 65° and 80° Celsius). Allow the holder to sit for five to ten minutes, then take it out with a potholder or oven mitt. Once the wax is soft, it may be removed with a paper towel.

Alternatively, you can use a hair dryer set on high to soften the wax. Hang on to the holder with an oven mitt and blow high heat over the wax. Once it softens, you can scoop it out or wipe it off.

Leave Your Candle Remains at a Crossroads

Throughout history and in many cultures, crossroads (an intersection or where two or more roads meet) have been considered places of magic. When you leave your spell remains at a crossroads, you are sending it out in all directions to the wider world. Therefore, you can leave both things you wish to get rid of and things you want to send out into the world at these places. For example, if you are doing a cleansing candle, you can leave the remains at a crossroads so that all the negativity goes away from you. If you are doing a spell for success, you can also leave that at a crossroads to spread your success in all directions.

Above all, be conscious of whatever you leave at the crossroads. Some things have a bigger ecological footprint than others. Leaving the ashes from a burnt petition paper will have a small impact, but dumping plastic bags, glass candle holders, jars of honey, and other such items that don't break down naturally creates litter and will leave an ugly mess or have to be picked up by someone else and thrown into a dumpster anyway. The smaller the footprint of any remains you plan on leaving, the more they are likely to integrate with the crossroads and continue to do their work.

That said, you don't have to leave all the remains at the crossroads to get the desired effect that leaving them can have. A teaspoon of the remaining wax and herbs can easily be left in the center of an intersection and carry the energy of your spell where you need it to go. Trays can be cleaned and reused, glass can be recycled, natural items such as beeswax and herbs can be composted, and the rest can be disposed of however you wish.

If you wish to leave your spell remains at the crossroads, then you can take them as-is or wrap just the remaining wax and herbs (not the glass or tray) in a paper bag or natural cloth and leave the packet in the middle of a quiet intersection. Drop it off and walk away from it without looking back. If what you are working on is something you are getting rid of, leave it at an intersection far from your home. If you are working on something that you would like to bring to you, leave it at an intersection closer to your home.

Burying the Remains

If you have done some work to remove a heavy curse or banish something negative, you may want to bury the remains somewhere away from your home. Burying is a ritual that has a sense of permanence to it.

For extreme negativity, you may bury your candle remains in a graveyard to make sure the issue is "dead and gone" or to get an amiable spirit to assist with your cause. If you bury something in a graveyard, be sure to bury it with some payment to the spirits. Coins and alcohol are symbolic payments that will make the spirits there more inclined to assist you.

Make Talismans

If you are working with beeswax candles, you have the option of repurposing your wax into a talisman. Beeswax talismans let you carry the magic of your spell and keep the energy going.

With the heat of your hands or with a hair dryer, you can soften the wax and form it into symbols such as hearts or dollar signs and place these wax talismans on your altar or add a small piece of the wax to a mojo bag. You can also form the wax into a poppet and continue to work on a particular person.

How Long Does It Take a Spell to Work?

That depends on the circumstances surrounding the situation: If your situation is one where energy is already flowing in the right direction, it's common to see results very quickly. However, more challenging situations might require a longer time or even more than one spell to turn around. I was taught, as a general rule, to check if the spell is moving things forward by first looking at the reading from the flame, wax, and smoke; from there, if all is well, you may check for messages, movement, and manifestation. The reason for looking for these three signposts is to remind us that most spells don't manifest overnight and to keep a positive outlook even if results aren't immediate.

Messages

Look for a small positive sign (such as hearing a special song on the radio, seeing a word on a billboard, hearing a name, seeing a repeating number on a clock, or seeing a symbol of some kind) within a few days of completing your candle spell. These are messages from the Universe or your spirit guides, not from the source of your spell. In other words, if you are doing a love spell to attract a specific person, this will not be a message from the person; it will be something you see or hear out in the world that strongly reminds you of the person. Expect to experience strong synchronicity (meaningful coincidence) of some kind. For example, you might meet a person who has the same name or see the person's birthdate on a license plate.

If you are working on a general spell instead of a particular person, your message might be more symbolic. For example, finding a penny on the street indicates that your prosperity spell is working.

Movement

Look for movement toward your goal within a few weeks—that is, something that happens in the direction of your desired outcome or an improvement of some kind. Unlike a message, movement is something that comes from the source. For example, if you were doing a spell for a new job, movement would be a call to come in for an interview. Movement is not the full manifestation of what you want; it is just a step in the right direction.

Manifestation

Look for the full manifestation of your outcome within a few months. Sometimes when I say this, people panic, "You mean it's going to take three months to get to my goal?" The key word is *within* a few months. That means anytime between one and ninety days or so. If you have an uncomplicated situation, you will most likely see a quicker outcome, although, with the right spell work, I have seen even complicated situations turn around miraculously.

What If I Don't See One of These?

If at any point you are not seeing a message, movement, or the final manifestation within the specified time frame, the reality is that you probably have to go back and give the work more energy, employ a new strategy, light another candle, or do some more spiritual work around your situation.

Think about this: not every disease is cured with one dose of medicine; sometimes another dose is required and other times several are required ... and sometimes it takes a different kind of medicine altogether. The same is true for spiritual work.

If you find that your spell work is not producing results and would like to know more specific timing for your particular case or a spiritual assessment of how challenged the situation is, you can consult with your favorite divination tool or get a reading from a trusted reader or magical practitioner who can look into your particular situation from a spiritual perspective.

14

Creating Your Grimoire

If you're going to do something complicated, you should start by planning it out first. Nothing is worse than getting halfway through a spell and then having to run to the local metaphysical shop for the ingredient you must have but can't find in your house or stumbling through your spell words because you haven't clarified what you're going to say.

Before you get started, write down your plan on paper. There's another great reason to write down your candle spells as well, and it sounds extra-witchy and magical—you need to create a grimoire.

What's a Grimoire?

"Grimoire" is a fancy word for your spell book. Some people call it a "Book of Shadows" (because it is their secret formulary) or a "Book of Light" (because it's all about getting enlightened) but ultimately your grimoire is the place where you are going to record your spells for all of posterity, or at least have them written down so that when you rock that prosperity spell and want to do it again a year later to bring in even more money, you can remember exactly what you did.

The Basic Steps of a Candle Spell

The basic steps of a candle spell can be outlined as follows:

1. Write out your petition paper.
2. Write out your cheat sheet with your spell words.
3. Clear and prepare your altar space.
4. Dress and bless your candle.
5. Place the candle on the altar.
6. Focus your energy.
7. Speak your spell words and light the candle.
8. Snuff the candle when you go to sleep or leave the house.
9. Relight it when you awaken or come back home.
10. Burn the candle until it's complete.
11. Dispose of any remains.

You're going to do these basics with your spell, but since you've learned about some more complex elements to incorporate into your work, we're going to add those to your list for your advanced candle preparation.

First, find a beautiful book to be your grimoire. Yes, you *can* use a dollar store spiral notebook for your spell book, but is that really going to satisfy your inner wizard? I didn't think so. At the same time, I don't want you to *not* start your grimoire because you're saving up your money for that $600 journal bound in Corinthian leather and hand-sewn by elves in a forest glade under the Libra full moon. Start with a beautiful journal that you love to look at *and* fits in your budget. After you do that big prosperity spell, I promise you that you can copy over your notes into that elven-made wonder (and if you know where to get one, will you let me know?).

The Breakdown of Your Spell Plan

If you really want to bring your magic *up*, you have to commit to writing your spells *down*. Here's a basic format of what should be noted in your grimoire:

> Objective of spell
> Start date for spell
> End date for spell
> Spell ingredients used
> Petition paper words
> Spoken spell words
> Spell layout and plan
> Ritual notes
> Candle burning notes
> Spell results

So let's break down what you're going to write for each section:

Before You Get Started

Before you get started writing things down in your grimoire, it's a good idea to clarify what this spell will be for. First start by free writing, just getting your thoughts down in a separate journal or on a piece of paper (see chapter 4 for details about free writing before writing your spell). Once you've written your paragraph on paper, focus on the true intention of your spell work and then you're ready to write in your grimoire.

Objective of Spell

The first thing you're going to write in your grimoire is the objective of your spell. Make sure that your objective is written in the positive—write about what you want, not what you *don't* want. Instead of writing, "This is a spell to get my boss to stop picking on me;" write, "This is a spell to get my boss to respect me, see me in a positive light, and treat me in a friendly way." If you write your spell objective in the negative, your boss might stop picking on you, but it doesn't set a course for what your boss does *instead* of picking on you— and those things may be things that you also don't want. For example, he could ignore you, fire you, or be inappropriate with you. So, to avoid just trading one problem for another, state your spell objective in the positive so you get exactly what you want.

Make sure that your spell addresses a single topic. Writing a spell that incorporates too many different topics will make your spell work confused and diluted. For example, instead of setting the objective "I would like my boss to respect me and I would also like to start a small side business for extra money," it would be more effective to do these as two separate spells.

Start Date for Spell/End Date for Spell

The start and end dates for the spell are important as well. If you have the option of planning your spell in the future, you may want to choose a date that gives your spell some advantages, such as a certain day of the week, moon phase, astrological sign, or numerological date that supports your outcome.

Write the end date for your spell if you are planning a multi-day spell and would like to have it end on a specific day. If you don't have a specific date when you would like the spell to end, leave space to note when your spell ended after you are done with your spell so you can remember how long it took the candle to burn.

Spell Ingredients Used

This is the fun part, where you get to plan which candles, oils, herbs, stones, shells, and talismans will be used in your spell. Thinking about the candle, you'll want to consider style, color, and how long you will want it to burn. You will also want to choose the oils, herbs, and curios that go along with the intention of your spell. (See appendix I for information about herbs and oils, appendix II for information about gemstones, appendix III for information about shells, and appendix IV for information about talismans).

Petition Paper Words

This is the place where you will work out the exact words and format for your petition paper. Using your spell objective as a basis, you can rewrite your petition in a way that reflects your goals. It may be that your petition words simply restate your objective as a more personal "I" statement, but if there are any other people are involved, it is more powerful to include their names.

For example, in the spell that we have been using as an example, a powerful, straight-forward petition could be "John Smith respects me, sees me in a positive light, and treats me in a friendly way" or writing John Smith three times and then crossing it with your name three times in a criss-cross pattern. (See chapter 3 for more information about creating petition papers).

Don't forget the other details! You will also want to note any sigils or symbols included on your petition paper as well as any words, symbols, or sigils carved into your candle.

Spoken Spell Words

It's also helpful to work out the words you are going to speak before you start your spell. Writing these words down means you won't get stuck or tongue-tied when it comes time to light your candle.

You may be like me, preferring to speak spell words off the top of your head in the moment, but even then, at least having an idea of what you are going to say ahead of time will give you a place to start. It's also a good idea to write down the general words spoken if you want to do a successful spell again in the future.

If you are the kind of person who enjoys using formal words or a poem as spell words, you will have your rhyming couplets in your grimoire so you can read from them as you light your candle and set your spell into motion.

Spell Layout and Plan

This is where you map out your spell. Writing out your spell plan is great for thinking ahead and knowing what you will need before you get started. If you are going to be making the candles you'll be using for your spells, this is the place you can prepare for that too. Sometimes you might think that you have everything you need listed in the spell ingredients section but then as you plan it out, realize that you forgot one thing or come up with a brilliant addition to your list of materials.

If you're a visual person, this will be the most fun part of your grimoire planning, because you can draw out a map for your spell. I like to draw a top down layout of my spell, showing where I'm going to place my candles and if it's a moving candle spell, where they're going to move. I can show the patterns of the herbs I'm going to sprinkle and can note the color of the candles and which oils and herbs I'm going to put on which candles.

This map can not only be useful for pre-planning, but when your spell has completed and you've gotten great results, it will help you to remember what you did and design future spells that also use the best elements from your successful work.

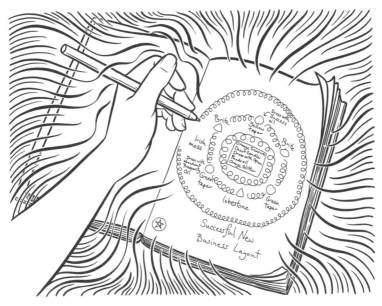

Example of a Spell Layout Map

Ritual Notes

If you are incorporating any rituals or special preparation for your spell, you may want to note that as well. Did you take a cleansing bath beforehand, for example, or burn a special incense in your room, or place a special cloth on your altar? Be sure to note these details in your grimoire as well.

Candle Burning Notes

While your candle is burning and once your candle is finished, you will want to note what happened. First, you will want to make any notes on how the candle was burning and any symbols you noted after the candle has completed. You can make your notes on pyromancy (reading the flame), ceromancy (reading the wax), and capnomancy (reading the smoke) as you go along and after the candle is finished, and relate them to the results that you get.

In this section, you can also note any troubleshooting you did on the candle to get it to burn well, such as pouring off excess wax or trimming the wick on a candle flame that was too high. In this section, you'll also want to note how you disposed of the candle remains, so that you can reference back to them later.

Spell Results

In this section, you will be jotting down the results of your spell and when the results happened. When a candle is complete, look for three signposts that give you feedback on how your spell is doing.

Messages are positive signs coming from the Universe about your spell.

Movement is something happening that indicates things are moving in the right direction, but that is not yet the final result of your spell.

Manifestation is the final result of your spell, achieving what it is that your spell set out to accomplish.

Noting the date at each step is important, because it gives you a reference point for how long the work took to manifest.

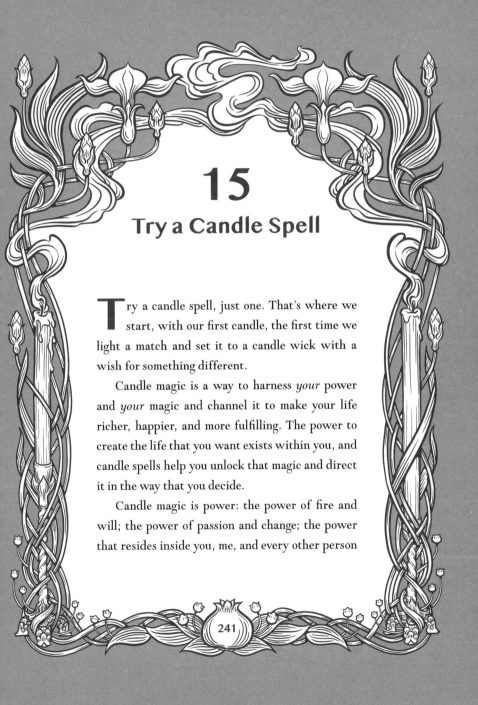

15

Try a Candle Spell

Try a candle spell, just one. That's where we start, with our first candle, the first time we light a match and set it to a candle wick with a wish for something different.

Candle magic is a way to harness *your* power and *your* magic and channel it to make your life richer, happier, and more fulfilling. The power to create the life that you want exists within you, and candle spells help you unlock that magic and direct it in the way that you decide.

Candle magic is power: the power of fire and will; the power of passion and change; the power that resides inside you, me, and every other person on this planet; the power that resides all around us and that we have access to at any moment, whenever we need it.

My mission was to show you, special and beautiful unique soul that you are, how to access the flame within you, harness the magic you hold inside you like a tiny flame, and how to feed that flame until it is the brightest light in the Universe.

Showing you how to create your own magic, showing you the magic that resides within you, and the magic that is all around you is my mission on this life journey. This book is a key to unlock all that magic.

Try a candle spell, just one, and you will start to feed the flame of power within. Work with candles, get to know them. Make friends with the petals, the herbs, the roots. Get your hands messy, covered with oils and glitter, covered with powders. Feel the power in your hands. Feel the power in your heart. Feel the power in your words as you let them flow out of you—out into the ether, into the heavens, back through time, and forward into the future—shifting, transmuting, bending the fabric of time and space to your will.

You have the power within you. Waiting to be unleashed. To transform yourself. To transform the world.

Try a candle spell, just one.

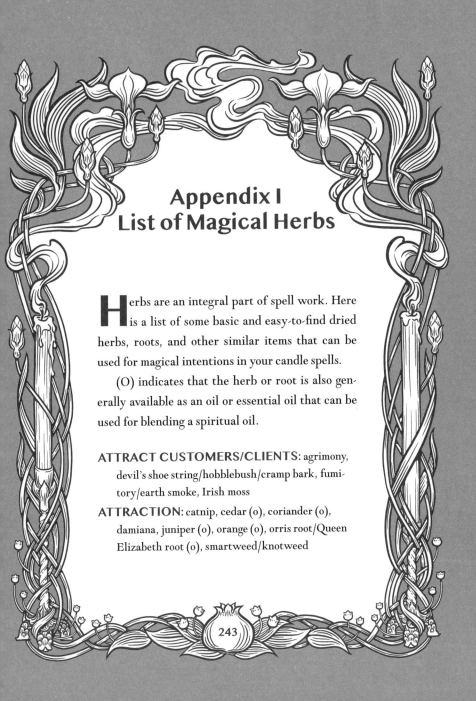

Appendix I
List of Magical Herbs

Herbs are an integral part of spell work. Here is a list of some basic and easy-to-find dried herbs, roots, and other similar items that can be used for magical intentions in your candle spells.

(O) indicates that the herb or root is also generally available as an oil or essential oil that can be used for blending a spiritual oil.

ATTRACT CUSTOMERS/CLIENTS: agrimony, devil's shoe string/hobblebush/cramp bark, fumitory/earth smoke, Irish moss

ATTRACTION: catnip, cedar (o), coriander (o), damiana, juniper (o), orange (o), orris root/Queen Elizabeth root (o), smartweed/knotweed

AUTHORITY: bergamot (o), jalap root/High John the Conqueror, masterwort root/master root, orris root/Queen Elizabeth root (o), Solomon's seal root, woodruff/master of the woods

BANISHING: asafoetida (o), barberry, bay laurel/bay leaf (o), boldo, cedar (o), devil's shoe string/hobblebush/cramp bark, knotweed, salt (black), valerian/vandal root (o)

BEAUTY: catnip, elecampane (o), ginseng (o), rosemary (o), yerba santa

BLESSING: angelica root (o), cedar (o), copal (o), frankincense (o), passionflower

BREAK BAD HABITS: eucalyptus (o), hyssop (o), knotweed

BREAK UP: lemon (o), lemon verbena (o), red pepper, salt (black), sulfur, trillium root/Beth root/Southern John root

BUSINESS SUCCESS: agrimony, alfalfa, allspice, bayberry, benzoin (o), cinnamon, cinquefoil/five finger grass, fumitory/earth smoke, Irish moss, sassafras (o), woodruff/master of the woods

CAREER: cinquefoil/five finger grass, grains of paradise, gravel root, mistletoe, pecan, woodruff/master of the woods

COMMUNICATION: deer's tongue

CONFUSION: black mustard seed (o), grains of paradise, poppy seed, red pepper, salt (black), sulfur

CONTROL OVER OTHERS: angelica (o), calamus root (o), cedar (o), ginseng (o), knotweed, licorice, mullein, quassia, tobacco

COURAGE: borage, mullein, tea, thyme (o), yarrow (o)

COURT CASES/LEGAL ISSUES: black mustard seed (o), buckthorn, calendula, cascara sagrada, cinquefoil/five finger grass, dill seed (o), galangal/Little John root (o), oregano (o), poppy seed

CURSING/JINXING/CROSSING: asafoetida (o), black mustard seed (o), black pepper (o), chicory, grains of paradise, red pepper, salt (black), sulfur, tobacco, valerian/vandal root (o)

DREAM WORK: camphor (o), celery seed (o), chamomile (o), cinquefoil/five finger grass, flax (o), frankincense (o), hibiscus, jasmine (o), rosemary (o), star anise (o)

EVIL EYE (PROTECTION FROM): agrimony, anise (o), cumin seed (o), devil's shoe string/hobblebush/cramp bark, elderflower, lemon, rue

FALL OUT OF LOVE: black walnut, pistachio

FAME: jalap root/High John the Conqueror, masterwort/master root, orris-root/Queen Elizabeth root, passionflower, sunflower (O)

FERTILITY: black mustard seed (o), fig, hawthorn, myrtle, patchouli (o), pine (o), white oak, yellow dock/dock

FIDELITY: basil (o), comfrey, cumin seed (o), hawthorn, magnolia, periwinkle, raspberry leaf, rosemary (o), senna, skullcap, spikenard (o), trillium root/Beth root/Southern John root

GOSSIP (ENDING): chia seed, clove (o), oregano (o), slippery elm

HAPPINESS: allspice (o), basil (o), benzoin (o), cacao beans, catnip, lavender (o), marjoram (o), thyme (o), vanilla

HEALING (EMOTIONAL): balm of Gilead, marjoram (o), vanilla

HEALING (GENERAL): allspice (o), althaea, angelica root (o), calamus root (o), caraway (o), coltsfoot, goldenseal, grains of paradise, lemon balm (o), myrrh (o), rue, sunflower (o)

HEALTH/STRENGTH: acorn, bay laurel/bay leaf (o), coriander (o), dill seed (o), jalap root/High John the Conqueror, peony, pine (o, salt (red), thyme, white oak, white sage (o)

IMMORTALITY: acacia, apple, sage (o), tansy

LOANS: alfalfa, cinquefoil/five finger grass, jalap root/High John the Conqueror, orris root/Queen Elizabeth root, Solomon's seal root

LOVE (NEW): cardamom (o), catnip, coriander (o), cubeb (o), lemon balm (o), lovage, sandalwood (o), senna, trillium root/Beth root/Southern John root

LOVE (PLATONIC): acacia, catnip, clove (o), passionflower

LOVE (ROMANTIC): American mandrake root/mayapple, caraway (o), catnip, cinnamon (o), cumin (o), damiana, deer's tongue, dill seed (o), dragon's blood, elecampane (o), gentian, ginger (o), hibiscus, jalap root/High John the Conqueror, jasmine (o), lavender (o), lemongrass (o), lovage, marjoram (o), myrtle (o), orris root/Queen Elizabeth root (O), passionflower, patchouli (o), red clover, rose (o), saffron, salt (pink), sandalwood (o), tonka bean (o), vanilla, violet leaf, yellow mustard seed (o)

LUCK (GAMBLING): alfalfa, allspice (o), angelica (o), arrowroot, calendula, chamomile (o), cinnamon (o), clove (o), comfrey, devil's shoe string/hobblebush/cramp bark, five finger grass, ginger (o), grains of paradise, Irish moss, jalap root/High John the Conqueror, Job's Tears, mistletoe, nutmeg (o)

LUCK (GENERAL): acorn, alkanet, basil (o), benzoin (o), calamus root (o), catnip, cumin (o), devil's shoe string/hobblebush/cramp bark, ginger (o), gravel root, jalap root/High John the Conqueror, pennyroyal, peony, salt (pink), salt (white), saltpeter, star anise (o), trillium root/Beth root/Southern John root

MARRIAGE: blood root, caraway (o), coriander (o), deer's tongue, hawthorn, lavender (o), magnolia, marjoram (o), myrtle (o), orange (o), periwinkle, raspberry leaf, red clover, rosemary (o), spikenard (o), trillium root/Beth root/Southern John root

MENTAL WELLNESS/CLARITY: cacao beans, caraway (o), coltsfoot, mustard seed (o), periwinkle, rosemary (o), rue, smartweed, spearmint (o)

NEW VENTURES: acorn, cinnamon (o), ginger (o), lemon balm (o), lemongrass (o)

PEACE: allspice (o), basil (o), benzoin (o), blood root, comfrey, cornflower, lavender (o), marjoram (o), myrrh (o), pennyroyal, periwinkle, rosemary (o), sandalwood (o), valerian/vandal root (o)

PERSONAL POWER: bergamot (o), carnation (o), devil's shoestring, echinacea/purple coneflower/sampson snake root, gentian, ginger (o), jalap root/High John the Conqueror, masterwort/master root, orris root/Queen Elizabeth root (o)

PROSPERITY/MONEY: acorn, alfalfa, alkanet, allspice (o), basil (o), bayberry, blue flag root, calendula, cascara sagrada cinnamon (o), cinquefoil/five finger grass, clove (o), comfrey, dragon's blood, fenugreek (o), ginger (o), Irish moss, nutmeg (o), patchouli (o), pine (o), sarsaparilla, sassafras (o), skullcap, smartweed

PROTECTION (GENERAL): acacia, agrimony, althaea, angelica (o), balm of gilead, barberry, basil (o), bay laurel/bay leaf (o), benzoin (o), black pepper (o), blessed thistle, blue cohosh, calamus root (o), cascara sagrada, cinquefoil/five finger grass, coriander (o), devil's shoe string/hobblebush/cramp bark, dragon's blood, elderflower, eucalyptus (o), fennel (o), feverfew, flax (o), ginger (o), grains of paradise, lemon (o), lemongrass (o), marjoram (o), mistletoe, mullein, mustard seed (o), myrrh (o), oregano (o), pennyroyal, peony, pine (o), poke, rue, salt (pink), salt (red), salt (white), sandalwood (o), slippery elm, Solomon's seal, trillium root/Beth root/Southern John root, verbena (o), white sage (o)

PROTECTION (MONEY): alkanet, chamomile (o), dragon's blood, peppermint (o), sassafras (o), spearmint (o)

PROTECTION (SPIRITS): angelica (o), anise (o), asafoetida (o), basil (o), bay laurel (o), caraway (o), dragon's blood, elder, frankincense (o), holly, mistletoe, pine (o), rue, star anise (o), white oak

PSYCHIC ABILITIES: acacia, althaea, anise (o), bay laurel/bay leaf (o), camphor (o), celery seed (o), cinnamon (o), coltsfoot, dandelion, flax (o), gravel root, jasmine (o), mugwort (o), peppermint (o), spearmint (o)

RECONCILIATION: balm of Gilead, basil (o), cornflower, damiana, dragon's blood, forget-me-not, spikenard (o)

REMOVING OBSTACLES: devil's shoe string/hobblebush/cramp bark, lemon balm (o), lemongrass (o), pine (o), salt (white)

REPEL ENEMIES: barberry, bay laurel (o), black pepper (o), eucalyptus (o), peppermint (o), red pepper, salt (black), spearmint (o), sulfur, valerian/vandal root (o)

REVENGE: asafoetida (o), black mustard seed (o), black pepper (o), grains of paradise, jalap root/High John the Conqueror, red pepper, salt (black), sulfur, tobacco, valerian/vandal root (o)

REVERSING CURSES: agrimony, asafoetida (o), devil's shoe string/hobble-bush/cramp bark, epsom salts, eucalyptus (o), lemongrass (o), rue, salt (black), vetiver, white sage (o)

SELF-CONFIDENCE: bergamot (o), cinquefoil/five finger grass, echinacea/purple coneflower/sampson snake root, ginger (o), jalap root/High John the Conqueror, orris root/Queen Elizabeth root, tobacco, yarrow (o)

SEX/LUST: blood root, calamus root (o), caraway (o), cardamom (o), celery seed (o), cinnamon (o), cubeb (o), damiana, dragon's blood, echinacea/purple coneflower/sampson snake root, ginger (o), hibiscus, jalap/High John the Conqueror, juniper (o), lemongrass (o), myrrh (o), patchouli (o), safflower (o), salt (red), sandalwood (o), sarsaparilla, yellow mustard seed (o)

SPIRIT WORK (CONNECTION TO SPIRITS): acacia, althaea, anise (o), balm of Gilead, cascara sagrada, celery seed (o), copal, dandelion, frankincense (o), grains of paradise, holly, sweetgrass, thistle, tobacco, wormwood (o)

SPIRITUAL CLEANSING/UNCROSSING: agrimony, alkanet, angelica root (o), anise (o), asafoetida (o), bay laurel/bay leaf (o), benzoin (o), blue cohosh, calamus root (o), camphor (o), chamomile (o), cinnamon (o), cinquefoil/five finger grass, dill seed (o), dragon's blood, feverfew, galangal/Little John root (o), hyssop (o), lemon balm (o), lemon verbena (o), lemongrass (o), nettle, patchouli (o), pennyroyal, peony, peppermint (o), pine (o), poke, rosemary (o), rue, salt (pink), salt (white), saltpeter, slippery elm, solomon's seal, spearmint (o), sulfur, valerian/vandal root (o), verbena (o), white oak, white sage (o)

SUCCESS/VICTORY: cinnamon (o), clover, echinacea/purple coneflower/sampson snake root, ginger (o), jalap root/High John the Conqueror, lemon balm (o), masterwort/master root, orris root/Queen Elizabeth root, sunflower (o), woodruff/master of the woods

TRAVEL SAFETY: cinquefoil/five finger grass, comfrey, mugwort (o), rue, thistle

WISDOM: bay laurel/bay leaf (o), Solomon's seal, sunflower (o), white sage (o)

WISHES: bay laurel/bay leaf (o), buckthorn, dandelion, elderflower, fava bean/ mojo bean, ginseng, grains of paradise, Job's Tears, sage (o), sandalwood (o), sunflower (o), tonka bean (o)

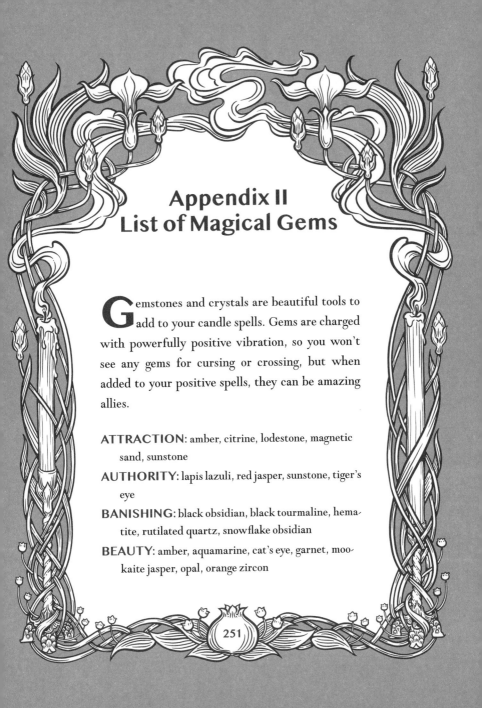

Appendix II
List of Magical Gems

Gemstones and crystals are beautiful tools to add to your candle spells. Gems are charged with powerfully positive vibration, so you won't see any gems for cursing or crossing, but when added to your positive spells, they can be amazing allies.

ATTRACTION: amber, citrine, lodestone, magnetic sand, sunstone

AUTHORITY: lapis lazuli, red jasper, sunstone, tiger's eye

BANISHING: black obsidian, black tourmaline, hematite, rutilated quartz, snowflake obsidian

BEAUTY: amber, aquamarine, cat's eye, garnet, mookaite jasper, opal, orange zircon

BREAK BAD HABITS: amethyst, black onyx, hematite

BUSINESS SUCCESS: bloodstone, citrine, green tourmaline, jade, malachite, pyrite, sunstone, yellow zircon

CAREER: garnet, lapis lazuli, malachite, sunstone

COMMUNICATION: apatite, aventurine, carnelian, celestite, howlite, rhodonite, sapphire, sardonyx, sodalite, turquoise

COURAGE: agate, amazonite, amethyst, aquamarine, bloodstone, blue goldstone, carnelian, diamond, howlite, lapis lazuli, mahogany obsidian, red tourmaline, rhodonite, tiger's eye, turquoise

CREATIVITY: amazonite, apatite, aventurine, malachite, red goldstone, sodalite

DREAM WORK: amethyst, azurite, blue calcite, Herkimer diamond, labradorite

EVIL EYE (PROTECTION FROM): black tourmaline, clear quartz, hematite, labradorite

FAME: aventurine, carnelian, malachite, red jasper, sunstone, yellow topaz

FIDELITY: dalmatian stone, garnet, morganite, opalite, turquoise

HAPPINESS: amethyst, angelite, aventurine, black onyx, carnelian, chrysoprase, rhodochrosite, yellow zircon

HEALING (EMOTIONAL): aventurine, chrysoprase, jade, lapis lazuli, prehnite, rhodonite, rose quartz, ruby fuchsite, sapphire, sodalite

HEALING (GENERAL): amethyst, azurite, blue calcite, cat's eye, celestite, clear quartz, hematite, lepidolite, moss agate, peridot

HEALTH/STRENGTH: agate, amber, beryl, bloodstone, calcite, carnelian, citrine, diamond, garnet, jet, red jasper, red zircon, sunstone, topaz

LOVE (NEW): lodestone, magnetic sand, rose quartz, tourmaline

LOVE (PLATONIC): agate, carnelian, chrysoprase, dalmatian stone, pink tourmaline, rose quartz, turquoise

LOVE (ROMANTIC): amber, amethyst, beryl, carnelian, garnet, jade, lapis lazuli, lepidolite, malachite, moonstone, pearl, rhodocrosite, sapphire, topaz

LUCK (GAMBLING): aventurine, cat's eye, lodestone, magnetic sand, pyrite, tiger's eye

LUCK (GENERAL): agate, amber, apache tear, aventurine, black tourmaline, chrysoprase, citrine, jet, lepidolite, olivine, opal, pearl, tourmalinated quartz, turquoise

MARRIAGE: dalmatian stone, diamond, emerald, ruby

MENTAL WELLNESS/CLARITY: aventurine, clear quartz, emerald, fluorite, hematite, labradorite, selenite, sodalite, zircon

NEW VENTURES: amazonite, blue kyanite, chrysoprase, moonstone

PAST LIVES: phantom quartz

PEACE: amethyst, angelite, aquamarine, aventurine, blue calcite, blue tourmaline, carnelian, chrysocolla, diamond, fluorite, lepidolite, malachite, obsidian, rhodochrosite, rose quartz, ruby fuchsite, sapphire, selenite, sodalite

PERSONAL POWER: lapis lazuli, sunstone, tiger's eye

PROSPERITY/MONEY: aventurine, bloodstone, calcite, cat's eye, chrysoprase, citrine, emerald, green tourmaline, green zircon, jade, lodestone, magnetic sand, malachite, moss agate, opal, pearl, peridot, pyrite, ruby, sapphire, sunstone, tiger's eye, topaz

PROTECTION (GENERAL): agate, amber, apache tear, black tourmaline, calcite, carnelian, chrysoprase, garnet, hematite, jasper, lapis lazuli, lepidolite, mahogany obsidian, malachite, mica, obsidian, olivine, onyx, red tourmaline, red zircon, ruby, snowflake obsidian, sunstone, tiger's eye, topaz

PROTECTION (MONEY): citrine, diamond, emerald, jade, moss agate, peridot, pyrite

PROTECTION (SPIRITS): black tourmaline, cat's eye, clear quartz, clear zircon, fluorite, jet, moonstone, pearl, peridot, shungite, smoky quartz, turquoise

PSYCHIC ABILITIES: amethyst, apatite, aquamarine, azurite, beryl, citrine, clear quartz, emerald, fluorite, garnet, herkimer diamond, labradorite, lapis lazuli, moonstone, prehnite, selenite, sodalite

RECONCILIATION: chrysoprase, diamond, rhodonite, selenite

REMOVING OBSTACLES: agate, clear quartz, fluorite, malachite

REPEL ENEMIES: black obsidian, black tourmaline, bloodstone, hematite

REVERSING CURSES: black tourmaline

SELF-CONFIDENCE: apatite, blue goldstone, iolite, pyrite red goldstone, red jasper, unakite

SEX/LUST: carnelian, garnet, red jasper, smoky quartz, sunstone, yellow zircon

SPIRIT WORK (CONNECTION TO SPIRITS): amethyst, angelite, boji stones, calcite, diamond, fluorite, Herkimer diamond, labradorite, lapis lazuli, lemurian seed crystal, lepidolite, mahogany obsidian, spirit amethyst, spirit quartz, sugilite

SPIRITUAL CLEANSING/UNCROSSING: aquamarine, black tourmaline, calcite, fluorite, snowflake obsidian

SUCCESS/VICTORY: amazonite, black onyx, blue goldstone, chrysoprase, lapis lazuli, lodestone, pyrite

TRAVEL SAFETY: aquamarine, chalcedony, moonstone, orange zircon

WISDOM: black onyx, chrysocolla, howlite, jade, lapis lazuli, prehnite, serpentine, sodalite, sugilite

WISHES: clear quartz

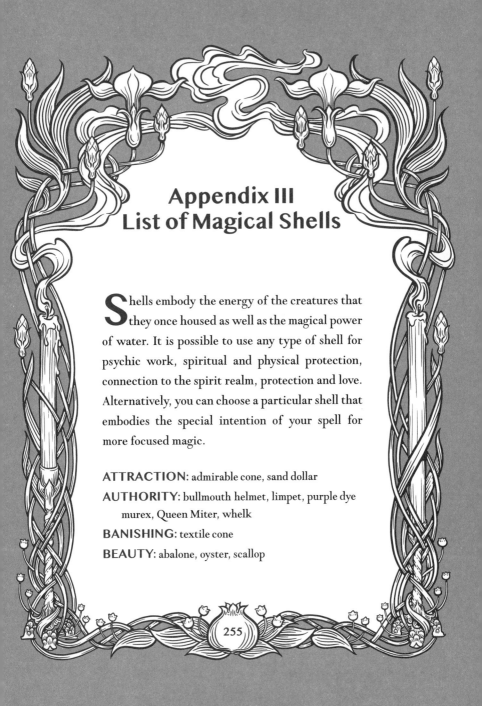

Appendix III
List of Magical Shells

Shells embody the energy of the creatures that they once housed as well as the magical power of water. It is possible to use any type of shell for psychic work, spiritual and physical protection, connection to the spirit realm, protection and love. Alternatively, you can choose a particular shell that embodies the special intention of your spell for more focused magic.

ATTRACTION: admirable cone, sand dollar

AUTHORITY: bullmouth helmet, limpet, purple dye murex, Queen Miter, whelk

BANISHING: textile cone

BEAUTY: abalone, oyster, scallop

BREAK BAD HABITS: lightning whelk, limpet, squamose chiton, warted egg cowrie

BUSINESS SUCCESS: cowrie, Polynesian Harp, top snail

CAREER: top snail, whelk

COMMUNICATION: clam, conch, cuttlefish bone, nude thorny oyster, olive, pencil urchin, tooth, triton

COURAGE: auger, cerith, leafy jewel box, limpet murex, reticulated cowrie helmet, tiger cowrie

CREATIVITY: moon snail, olive, thorny oyster, triton, wentletrap, whelk

DIVINATION: cowrie

EVIL EYE (PROTECTION FROM): cat's eye, coral

FAME: illustrious cone, sundial, thorny oyster

FERTILITY: cerith, coral, cowrie, oyster scallop, seahorse, whelk egg case

FIDELITY: cowrie

FREEDOM: angel wing, turkey wing

GOSSIP (ENDING): cat's eye, lion's paw scallop, rapa snail, snipe's bill murex, thorny oyster

HAPPINESS: cockle, grinning tun, Japanese Babylon, triton, turkey wing

HEALING (EMOTIONAL): chick pea cowrie, cockle, red abalone, sand dollar, spindle, turkey wing

HEALING (GENERAL): abalone, clam, nautilus, olive, sand dollar, scallop, screw

HEALTH/STRENGTH: auger, bear's paw, clam, conch, helmet, limpet, lion's paw, nautilus, oyster, spider

LEGAL MATTERS: foliated thorn murex

LOVE (NEW): oyster

LOVE (PLATONIC): bear's paw, cockle, conch, kitten's paw oyster, onion, periwinkle

LOVE (ROMANTIC): clam, cockle, cowrie, scallop, spindle

LUCK (GENERAL): coral, oyster, sand dollar, whelk

MARRIAGE: cowrie, noble frog, wedding cake venus clam

MENTAL WELLNESS/CLARITY/FOCUS: auger, conch, leopard cone, nautilus, paper moon scallop, periwinkle, sand dollar, whelk

NEW VENTURES: cockle, conch, hieroglyphic venus clam, keyhole limpet, little star bolma, nautilus, olive sundial

PEACE: abalone, cockle, janthina, jingle, miter, moon shell, sand dollar, scallop, sundial

PERSONAL POWER: bear's paw, limpet, spider, thorned latirus, top snail, tusk shell

PROSPERITY/MONEY: abalone, candy-stripe tree snail, clam, cowrie, janthina, olive, oyster, sand dollar, slipper tooth shell

PROTECTION (GENERAL): ark, auger, bear's paw, cone, helmet, moon snail, murex, mussel, slipper, spider, thorny oyster

PROTECTION (FROM SPIRITS): abalone, cat's eye, coral

PSYCHIC ABILITIES: abalone, cowrie, janthina, jingle, limpet, moon snail

RECONCILIATION: cowrie (blue)

REMOVING OBSTACLES: angel wing, cat's eye, frog conch, limpet

SELF-CONFIDENCE: cerith, clam, drupe, limpet, lion's paw, reticulated cowrie helmet, venus comb murex

SEPARATION: carrier

SEX/LUST: auger, cowrie (blue), oyster

SPIRIT WORK (CONNECTION TO SPIRITS): angel wing, crown conch, miter, sand dollar, scallop, spire

SPIRITUAL CLEANSING/UNCROSSING: abalone, clam, conch, olive shell

STABILITY: ark, clam, cowrie, helmet, mussel, periwinkle, top snail

APPENDIX III

SUCCESS/VICTORY: angel wing, blood mouth conch, cerith, Glory of India cone, limpet, lion's paw, murex, tooth shell, triumphant star tusk shell

TRAVEL: scallop

WISDOM: conch, limpet, sand dollar, whelk

WISHES: Placostylus land snail

Appendix IV
List of Magical Talismans

Talismans can be added to an altar or placed around a candle to bring in support for spell work. Talismans can be the actual item (for example, an acorn) or a symbol of the item (a silver charm shaped like an acorn).

ACORN: new beginnings building to great success, savings, fertility, luck

ANKH: everlasting life, past lives, success

ARROWHEAD: movement, action, direction, protection; virility, focus, new love

BANKNOTES: prosperity and long-term wealth

BEAD: beauty, adornment, wealth

BEE: fertility, community, success in seemingly impossible circumstances, abundance, cooperation, sweetness, joy, successful endeavors, beauty

BELL: clairaudience, spirit messages, element of air, communication

BONES: ancestors, divination, grounding, strength, indestructibility, healing

BUCKEYE: health, protection, prosperity (toxic if eaten—keep away from pets and children)

BREAD: life, health, abundance, gratitude, friendship, family, marriage

BUTTON: sealing, binding, connecting

CAULDRON: transformation, magic, divination, rebirth, abundance

CHALICE: spirit, emotions, spirituality, psychic awareness

COINS: prosperity, or if from another country, can attract travel opportunities

CORNUCOPIA: abundance, prosperity, health, wishes

DICE: luck in chancy situations, luck when the odds are against you, gambling luck, the side facing up can be chosen for numerological significance

DOLL: representation of an individual

DOMINO: gambling luck, luck against the odds, the domino chosen can be selected for numerological significance.

EGG: immortality, fertility, abundance, protection against the evil eye, cleansing.

EVIL EYE CHARM: a charm with blue and white concentric circles, for protection against jealous glances and negativity coming from others.

EYE OF HORUS: health, strength, protection

FEATHER: air, sky gods, angels, freedom, travel

FISH: water, psychic ability, emotional balance, love

FOSSIL: past lives, history, Akashic records, ancestors

FOUR-LEAF CLOVER: luck, health, wealth, happiness, love

FROG: abundance, fertility, luck, love, water

HAG STONE: a stone with a natural hole. Protection, healing, psychic visions

HAMSA HAND: good luck, happiness, protection against negativity and jealous people

HEART: romantic love, platonic love, health, joy

HORN: sexuality, vigor, abundance, fertility

HORSESHOE: good luck, protection from mischievous spirits

INCENSE BURNER: connection to Spirit, cleansing, imbuing

INDIAN HEAD PENNY: protection from law enforcement

IRON KEY: unlocking of good luck, easy delivery of baby, opening of doors, freedom, key to one's heart, keys of knowledge, protection from troublesome spirits, opening psychic awareness

ITALIAN HORN (CORNICELLO): good luck and protection from jealousy and negativity

KNIFE (ATHAME): cutting, ending, thought, ideas, communication

KNOT: binding, sealing, blocking, controlling, dominating, marriage, union, agreements, contracts

LADDER: spiritual ascension, connection between worlds, ancestors, angels

LOCK: binding, controlling, commitment

LODESTONE: good luck, love, prosperity, attraction

LOTUS: fertility, motherhood, enlightenment, prosperity, beauty, purity

MAGNET: attraction of all good things, manifestation, sexual chemistry

MERCURY DIME: money protection, gambling luck, communication

MILAGROS: blessings depending on the symbolism of the charm

MIRROR: reflection, reversing, self-love, spirit, psychic awareness

NAIL: protection, force, banishing, destruction

OUROBOROS: infinity, cycles, unity, renewal

OWL: wisdom, wealth, luck, transformation, spirit messages

PERSONAL CONCERNS: items that connect a spell to a particular person. Personal concerns can be hair, bodily fluids, fingernail clippings, signatures, objects owned by the person or anything with the person's DNA on it.

PINECONE: fertility, prosperity

PRISM: promises, protection, diversity, immortality, reincarnation, joy, happiness, prosperity

RABBIT'S FOOT: good luck charm, spirit contact

RELIGIOUS MEDALS: blessings and protection from the deity or saint depicted

RING: marriage, proposal, union, ongoing success and happiness

RUNE: each rune has a particular energy that can be used as a talisman

SCARAB: protection, good luck, creation, reincarnation, transformation

SKULL CHARM: thoughts, ideas, mental health, mental clarity, ancestors

TAROT CARDS: each card has a particular energy that can be used as a talisman

WISHBONE: luck, wishes coming true, victory in competitive situations

WITCH BALL: protection from evil spirits

YIN AND YANG: duality, harmony, wholeness

ZODIAC SYMBOLS: each symbol has the particular energy of that sign and can be used as a talisman representing the characteristics of the sign or a person with that sun sign

Appendix V
List of Symbols

This is by no means a complete list of possible symbols but touches on some common symbols and their meanings and can give you an idea on how to interpret the more unusual symbols that may show up for you as you do candle reading.

ACORN: good fortune, financial gain, beginnings of success, great ideas

ANCHOR: good luck, stability, hope

ANGEL: spirit guides, good news, protection

ANT: productivity, working as a group, getting things done step-by-step

APPLE: long life, success, abundance, love, commitment, temptation

ARCHWAY: passing into a new phase, graduation, higher levels

ARROWS: focus, reaching goals, pay attention

AXE: problems overcome, effort produces results

BABY: pregnancy, new creative projects, joyful beginnings

BALLOON: celebrations, happiness, play

BED: rest, sex, healing, meditation, let it go

BELL: unexpected good news, pay attention, synchronicities

BIRDS: good luck, travel, communication

BOAT: distant travel, overcoming the ups and downs of life

BONES: ancestors, spirit guides, past lives

BOOK: education, learning, school, writing

BOTTLE: celebration, escape from reality, addiction

BOUQUET: good luck, marriage proposals, loving friends, success, happy love life

BOWL: generous friends, spirit work

BRIDGE: travel, moving on, long-distance connections, opportunities

BUSH: minor financial or career improvement

BUTTERFLY: beauty, rebirth, transformation, evolution, major positive changes

CANDLE: enlightenment, magic, guidance

CAR: wealth, movement, partnership, short-distance travel

CASTLE: unexpected fortune, stability, long-lasting wealth, protection

CAT: independence, freedom, mystery, elusiveness

CHAIN: feeling trapped, burdens

CHAIR: house guests

CIGAR: wealth, success, celebration

CLOCK: time passing, waiting, patience

CLOUDS: not seeing the whole picture, confusion

CLOVER: very good luck, exceptional happiness, increase in prosperity

COFFIN: endings, transition, stillness

COIN: money, abundance, prosperity

COMB: beauty, glamour

COMPASS: business travel, distant travel

COW: prosperity, peace

CROSS: choices, x-ing out something, sacrifice

CROWN: success, honor, power, authority, achievement

DOG: loyalty, friendship, companionship

DOVE: faith, peace, promises, partnership, love

DRAGON: protection, wealth

EAGLE: moving, honor, success

EAR: listening, hearing important messages, clairaudience

EGG: wholeness, new projects

ELEPHANT: luck, good health

FACE: spirit guides, friends, allies

FENCE: being "on the fence," barriers, limitations that must be overcome

FISH: abundance, good news from another country, getting out of sticky situations

FLAG: warnings, pay attention to avoid problems, "red flags"

FORKED LINE: decisions, being at a crossroads, spiritual choices

FOX: craftiness, intellect, solutions come from thinking steps ahead

GOAT: virility, sensuality, health, hard work produces results

GRAPES: family abundance, happiness

GREYHOUND: decisiveness, quick action

GUN: protection, aggression

HAMMER: challenges overcome, hard work produces results

HAND: open hand means help from others, closed means self-reliance

HAT: success in life, keeping information "under your hat"

HEART: love, passion, friendship, happy family, pleasure

HOOK: addiction, obsession

HORSE: courage, success, sexual luck

HORSESHOE: luck, protection, safe travel

HOURGLASS: time is of the essence, decisions must be made

HOUSE: domesticity, happy home, new house

ICEBERG: freezing up, coldness, obstacles that must be avoided

ICICLE: communication needs thawing

JEWELS: expensive gifts, engagement, luxury

KETTLE: pay attention, heated words, passions running hot, visitors

KITE: seeing things from a bird's eye view, take a step back, wishes come true

KNIFE: separations, take care with communication, surgery resolves health issues

LADDER: promotion, social or career success

LEAF: new beginnings, starting a new life

LINES: movement, travel, separation, wavy lines mean a long and winding path, straight lines mean a direct and quick path

LION: influential friends, powerful people

LOCK: need for escape, obstacles to doors opening

MASK: insecurity

MOON: mysticism, dreams, magic

MOUNTAIN: power, obstacles, friends that you can rely on

MOUSE: protect belongings to prevent theft

MUSHROOM: fairy magic, otherworldly contact

NECKLACE: admirers, expensive gifts

OWL: wisdom, study, knowledge, school, wise advice

PEAR: social status, positive business move, fertility, sweetness

PEOPLE: friends, helpers, spirit guides

PIG: good luck, faithful lover

PINE TREE: prosperity, long life, steadfastness

PURSE: personal prosperity

QUESTION MARK: riddles, mystery, unresolved issues based on lack of communication

RABBIT: fertility, good luck, need for courage

RAT: secrets revealed, false friends

RING: engagement, marriage, promises, commitments

ROCKET: results exceed expectations

ROSE: true love, popularity

SAW: idle gossip, trouble from strangers, interference

SCALES: court cases, justice, balance, fairness

SCISSORS: break-up, cut and clear, arguments

SHEEP: prosperity, success, mildness

SHELL: psychic awareness, intuition

SHIP: successful journey

SNAKES: transformation, rebirth, immortality, healing

STAR: divine intervention, soul mates, hope, wishes coming true

SUN: fame, positive attention, recognition, achievement

SWAN: partnerships, commitment, love, marriage

SWORD: positive or negative communication, clarity

TREES: growth, financial abundance, stability, windfall

TURTLE: movement is slow and steady, longevity

UMBRELLA: protection from difficulties, bad situations turn around, shelter

UNICORN: mystical blessing, unique and unusual solutions

URN: messages from ancestors, past lives

VOLCANO: passions run hot, emotional outbursts

WATERFALL: powerful emotions, flowing prosperity

WHEEL: inheritance, change in fortunes

WINGS: spirit guide messages, guardian angels, escape

Glossary

ALTAR: a dedicated table for spellwork

ALTAR CANDLE: a candle for honoring a deity, saint, angel, or spirit

ARCANE: mysterious or secret

BOOKOFSHADOWS/ BOOK OF LIGHT: a book to note spells, spell words, and magical knowledge

BOTANICA: a small store selling religious and spiritual supplies

BEESWAX FOUNDA- TION: a sheet of beeswax with a hexagon pattern similar to the pattern bees make in their hives

CAPNOMANCY: reading and interpreting smoke symbolically

CEROMANCY: reading and interpreting wax symbolically

CHARGE: to infuse with spirit and magical power

CHARM BAG: a small cloth bag charm created with herbs and talismans for a magical purpose

COERCIVE MAGIC: spells meant to make another person do your will

CURIOS: rare and unusual magical item

CURSE: a spell meant to harm someone

DEITY: a god or goddess

DOUBLE-ACTION CANDLE: a large taper candle that is half one color and half black that is used in spells to send negativity back to its source

DRESSED AND BLESSED: a candle that has added oils and herbs and is blessed by the maker for a specific intention

ELEMENTS: the four classical elements: air, fire, water, earth and sometimes a fifth element of spirit

ENERGY: a spiritual intention which can flow from a person

ETERNAL FLAME: a candle used to light another candle

FAE: fairy

FIGURAL CANDLE: a candle in a shape that represents something symbolically

FIXED: a candle that is prepared with herbs and oils

FREE-WRITING: to write in a stream-of-consciousness style to organize thoughts

GRIMOIRE: a book to note spells, spell words, and magical knowledge

HELPER WICK: an extra piece of wick added to a candle when a wick is lost

HIGHER SELF: the most spiritually enlightened version of ourself

INSCRIBE: to carve words into wax

INTENTION: the goal of the spell

INVOKE: to invite in, to call on

JAR CANDLE: a wax candle encased in a glass jar

KARMA: the spiritual cause and effect of one's actions

LAYOUT: a visual map of a complex spell

MANIFESTATION: the real-world result of a spell

MASTER CANDLE: the main candle in a multi-candle spell

METAPHYSICAL STORE: a store selling religious and spiritual supplies

NOVENA: a nine-day prayer or candle

NUMEROLOGY: the spiritual significance of numbers

OCCULT: supernatural, mystical, or magical

PERSONAL CONCERNS: personal items added to spell work to link it to an individual. Usually something that contains the person's DNA, such as hair or a piece of worn clothing.

PETITION PAPER: a slip of paper with a wish or intention for the spell

PILLAR: a tall piece of wax drips that form a column

POPPET: a doll standing in for a person for magical purposes

PRACTITIONER: a person who does magic

PRIMED WICK: wick that has been dipped in wax to make it rigid for candle making

PULL-OUT: a vigil candle refill, a candle that can be placed in or taken out of a glass holder

PYROMANCY: reading and interpreting a flame or fire symbolically

REVERSE-ACTION: a red candle that is dripped with an outer coating of black wax used in reversing spells

REVERSING: to send negativity back to its source

RITUAL: a traditional set of a series of actions to perform magical work

ROAD OPENER: a spell used to push aside blocks

SEAL: a written or inscribed spiritual symbol for a particular magical purpose

SIGIL: a drawn or inscribed symbol for a particular magical purpose

SOOT: carbon build-up on a glass candle holder

SPELL BOTTLE: a bottle charm created with herbs and talismans for a magical purpose

SPELL CASTER: a person who casts spells or makes magic

SPELL CASTING: to send off a spell

SPELL WORK: to create spells and send them off

SPIRIT: the energy that connects all things

SPIRIT: the non-physical essence of a being

SPIRIT CANDLE: a candle for honoring a deity, saint, angel, or spirit

SPIRIT GUIDE: one of the spirits who surround us for help and guidance

SPIRITUAL OIL: an oil made with herbs and essential oils for a magical purpose

SPIRITUALIST: a person who contacts spirits

SUN FIRE: fire created with a magnifying glass concentrating the rays of the sun

SUPPORT CANDLE: a secondary candle that is used to bring extra energy to a main candle in a spell

SYMBOL: a representation that stands for something else

SYMPATHETIC MAGIC: using representative symbolic items to effect magic on someone at a distance

SYNCHRONICITY: a meaningful coincidence

TALISMAN: an item with magical powers

TAPER: a tall slim candle

TARGET: the person at whom the magic spell is directed

TRIPLE-ACTION CANDLE: a large taper candle with three colors divided in thirds

TUNNELING: when a candle burns down the center and leaves a shell on the outside

UNIVERSE: the energy that connects all things

VIGIL CANDLE: a candle in a tall glass cylinder-shaped holder

VISUALIZATION: holding an image in the mind's-eye

VOTIVE CANDLE: a small pillar candle placed in a small glass holder

WILL: the source of decisiveness and action

WITCH: a person who practices magic

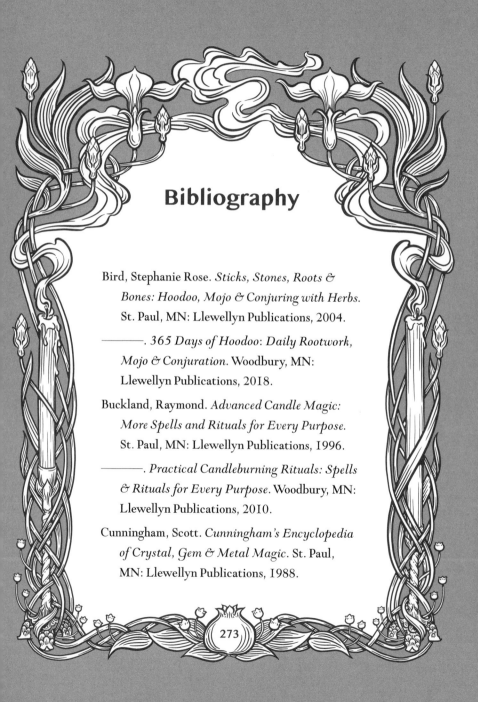

Bibliography

Bird, Stephanie Rose. *Sticks, Stones, Roots &
Bones: Hoodoo, Mojo & Conjuring with Herbs.*
St. Paul, MN: Llewellyn Publications, 2004.

———. *365 Days of Hoodoo: Daily Rootwork,
Mojo & Conjuration.* Woodbury, MN:
Llewellyn Publications, 2018.

Buckland, Raymond. *Advanced Candle Magic:
More Spells and Rituals for Every Purpose.*
St. Paul, MN: Llewellyn Publications, 1996.

———. *Practical Candleburning Rituals: Spells
& Rituals for Every Purpose.* Woodbury, MN:
Llewellyn Publications, 2010.

Cunningham, Scott. *Cunningham's Encyclopedia
of Crystal, Gem & Metal Magic.* St. Paul,
MN: Llewellyn Publications, 1988.

————. *Cunningham's Encyclopedia of Magical Herbs*. St. Paul, MN: Llewellyn Publications, 1985.

————. *Magical Aromatherapy: The Power of Scent*. St. Paul, MN: Llewellyn Publications, 1989.

Dey, Charmaine. *The Magic Candle*. Old Bethpage, NY: Original Publications, 1982.

Dow, Caroline. *Tea Leaf Reading for Beginners*. Woodbury, MN: Llewellyn Publications, 2011.

Fenton, Sasha. *Tea Cup Reading: A Quick and Easy Guide to Tasseography*. San Francisco: Weiser, 2002.

Foxwood, Orion. *The Candle and the Crossroads: A Book of Appalachian Conjure and Southern Root-Work*. San Francisco: Weiser, 2012.

Frater U.: D.:. *Practical Sigil Magic: Creating Personal Symbols for Success*. Woodbury, MN: Llewellyn Publications, 2012.

Gamache, Henri. *The Master Book of Candle Burning: How to Burn Candles for Every Purpose*. Old Bethpage, NY: Original Publications, 1998.

Hansen, Michelle. *Ocean Oracle: What Seashells Reveal About Our True Nature*. Hillsboro, OR: Beyond Words, 2007.

————. *Ocean Wisdom: Lessons from the Seashell Kingdom*. Hillsboro, OR: Beyond Words, 2007.

Harrison, Karen. *The Herbal Alchemist's Handbook: A Grimoire of Philtres, Elixirs, Oils, Incense, and Formulas for Ritual Use*. San Francisco: Weiser, 2011.

Illes, Judika. *The Encyclopedia of 5000 Spells: The Ultimate Reference Book for the Magical Arts*. New York: HarperOne, 2004.

————. *Encyclopedia of Witchcraft: The Complete A–Z for the Entire Magical World*. New York: HarperOne, 2005.

Kynes, Sandra. *Sea Magic: Connecting with the Ocean's Energy*. Woodbury, MN: Llewellyn Publications, 2008.

Lightfoot, Najah. *Good Juju: Mojos, Rites & Practices for the Magical Soul*. Woodbury, MN: Llewellyn Publications, 2019.

Mathers, Samuel Liddell MacGregor. *The Key of Solomon the King: Clavicula Salomonis*. San Francisco: Wesier, 2000.

Pajeon, Kala, and Ketz Pajeon. *The Candle Magick Workbook*. New York: Citadel Press, 1998.

Pepper, Elizabeth. *The ABC of Magic Charms*. Newport, RI: The Witches' Almanac, 2009.

Peterson, Joseph H., ed. *The Lesser Key of Solomon*. San Francisco: Weiser, 2001.

————. *The Sixth and Seventh Books of Moses*. Newburyport, MA: Ibis Press, 2008.

Picton, Margaret. *The Book of Magical Herbs: Herbal History, Mystery & Folklore*. New York: Barron's, 2000.

Riva, Anna. *Candle Burning Magic: A Spellbook of Rituals for Good and Evil*. Los Angeles: International Imports, 1980.

————. *Secrets of Magical Seals: A Modern Grimoire of Amulets, Charms, Symbols and Talismans*. Los Angeles: International Imports, 1975.

Robinett, Kristy. *Born Under a Good Sign: Make the Most of Your Astrological Sign*. Woodbury, MN: Llewellyn, 2019.

Smith, Jacki. *Coventry Magic with Candles, Oils, and Herbs*. San Francisco: Weiser, 2011.

Theodore, K.P. *The Fundamental Book of Sigil Magic*. Glasgow, Scotland, UK: Erebus Society, 2018.

Towers, Jacqueline. *Tea Leaf Reading: Discover Your Fortune in the Bottom of a Cup*. Charlottesville, VA: Hampton Roads, 2018.

Yronwode, Catherine, and Mikhail Strabo. *The Art of Hoodoo Candle Magic in Rootwork, Conjure, and Spiritual Church Services*. Forestville, CA: Missionary Independent Spiritual Church, 2013.

———. *Hoodoo Root and Herb Magic: A Materia Magica of African-American Conjure*. Forestville, CA: Lucky Mojo Curio Company, 2002.

Zakroff, Laura Tempest. *Sigil Witchery: A Witch's Guide to Crafting Magick Symbols* . Woodbury, MN: Llewellyn Publications, 2018.

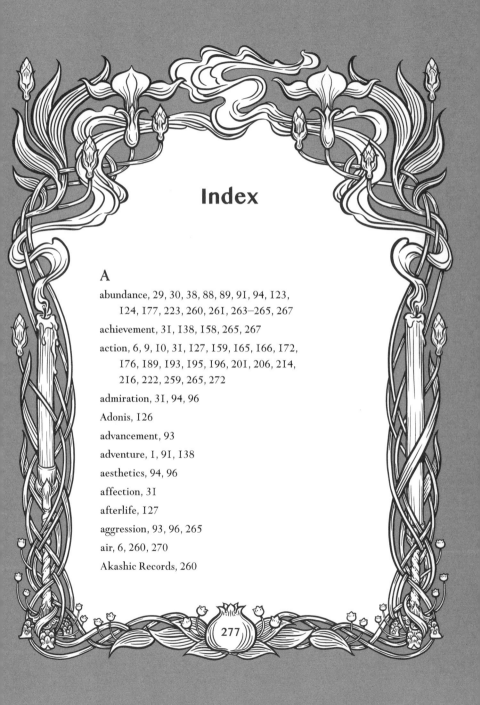

Index

C

E

F

G

I

M

magic, 1–3, 5, 6, 8–13, 15, 19, 21, 22, 24, 29–31, 33–42, 44, 47,
48, 50, 54, 56, 60, 63, 65–68, 73, 75, 79, 83, 88–90, 93, 94,
99, 100, 105, 108, 110, 112, 115, 117, 119–121, 123, 125,
126, 128, 130, 133, 135–139, 161, 164, 180, 190, 202, 207,
208, 217–221, 227, 229, 235, 241, 242, 255, 260, 264, 266,
270–272

    ceremonial, 121, 219

    coercive, 11, 270

    sex, 31, 94, 123, 126, 128, 264

    sympathetic, 75, 119, 120, 125, 272

magic squares of Abramelin, 63

magician, 1, 10, 128

magnetism, 30, 31

man, 125

manifestation, 1, 9, 10, 51, 67, 75, 138, 139, 141, 159, 161–164,
229–231, 240, 261, 270

marriage, 91–93, 96, 124, 138, 160, 246, 253, 257, 260–262, 264,
266, 267

Mary, 56, 126, 128

Mason jar, 177–180

master candle, 21, 22, 135, 136, 270

mastery, 31, 158

matches, 13, 16, 20, 33, 34, 71, 74, 80, 112, 115, 219

    fireplace, 34, 220

    kitchen, 34, 218

    paper, 24, 37, 40, 42, 47, 48, 50–58, 61, 63, 75, 78, 81, 84,
111–113, 115, 116, 118, 129, 178, 183, 184, 187, 208,
223, 224, 226–228, 233–238, 257, 271

material, 19, 36, 39, 43, 75, 76, 138, 158, 162–164, 166, 189, 193,
195, 201, 211, 224

mediation, 96

P

W

To Write to the Author

If you wish to contact the author or would like more information about this book, please write to the author in care of Llewellyn Worldwide Ltd. and we will forward your request. Both the author and publisher appreciate hearing from you and learning of your enjoyment of this book and how it has helped you. Llewellyn Worldwide Ltd. cannot guarantee that every letter written to the author can be answered, but all will be forwarded. Please write to:

Madame Pamita
℅ Llewellyn Worldwide
2143 Wooddale Drive
Woodbury, MN 55125-2989

Please enclose a self-addressed stamped envelope for reply,
or $1.00 to cover costs. If outside the U.S.A., enclose
an international postal reply coupon.

Many of Llewellyn's authors have websites with additional information and resources. For more information, please visit our website at http://www.llewellyn.com